A Spectator's Guide to
World Religions

A Lion Book
an imprint of
Lion Hudson plc
Wilkinson House, Jordan Hill Road,
Oxford OX2 8DR, England
www.lionhudson.com
ISBN 978 0 8254 6252 8 (USA)
ISBN 978 0 7459 5308 3 (UK)

First published in 2004 by Blue Bottle Books, PO Box A287, Sydney,
South Australia 1235
First Lion edition 2008
10 9 8 7 6 5 4 3 2 1 0

A catalogue record for this book is available
from the British Library

Typeset in 11/13 Latin 725 BT
Printed and bound in the USA

A SPECTATOR'S GUIDE TO

WORLD RELIGIONS

An Introduction to the Big Five

JOHN DICKSON

LION

For Buff
the truest thing in my life.

Thank you

Cornay Sinac, for reading everything and reminding me to keep it clear and simple.

Duncan Giles, for influencing the direction of the book more than you know.

St Andrew's, for time to write and friendships for life.

Café Pio, for my second office and the best *doppio* in town.

Those who kindly read draft chapters and offered insights and corrections: Richard and Judy Schumack, Marie Graber, Dr Sheevalee Patel, Kelsang Sudhana, Simon Smart, Dr Kankesu Jayanthakumaran, Harry and Olive Cotter, and Simona Barukh.

All remaining inadequacies are my own.

Contents

Preface

The feast of ideas

My introduction to faith came not through family tradition, 'Sunday School', church, or any other formal means of religious instruction, but through the irresistible power of good food.

One of the relics of Australia's Christian heritage is the once-a-week Scripture lesson offered in many state high schools around the country. Usually, the person running the lesson was an elderly volunteer from the local church. I took my chances with these harmless old ladies because 'non-Scripture' involved doing homework under the supervision of a *real* teacher.

One of these Scripture teachers had the courage one day to invite the entire class to her home for discussions about 'God'. The invitation would have gone unnoticed, except that she added: 'Oh, and if anyone gets hungry, I'll be making hamburgers, milkshakes and scones.' Perhaps it was an unfair offer to a bunch of teenage blokes!

Several weeks later I was sitting on a comfy lounge in this woman's home with half a dozen classmates, feasting on her food and bracing myself for the 'God bit'. I had never been to church or even had a religious conversation of any length, so this was an entirely new experience. I remember thinking at the time that there was nowhere to run. I had eaten so much of her food I couldn't have left the couch if I'd tried.

My fears were unfounded. This lady's style was completely relaxed. She knew she was speaking to a room full of religious 'spectators' rather than players and so she never pushed us. She asked us what we thought, she let us ask her what she thought, and she read to us relevant parts of the Bible. For me and several others from that one class, this was the beginning of a very interesting journey into the wonders of faith.

Life has changed a lot since those days. Whereas I once prided myself on 'not being the religious type', I suppose now I appear about as 'religious' as a modern Australian can get.

I've recorded songs about faith, written books about it, given talks on it, completed degrees in it, and even went so far as to get myself ordained as a Christian minister.

And yet, for all this 'religion' in my life I still wince when people ask: 'Are you *religious*?' It's not that I'm embarrassed about spirituality – far from it – it's just that the word 'religion' sometimes conjures up images of formality, close-mindedness and strictness, and these are the last descriptions I'd attach to my current faith.

I guess those early hamburger discussions as a teenager set the course of my spiritual journey in subtler ways than simply convincing me of the merits of Christ. Whether in song, speech or print I have always felt more in tune with religious 'spectators' than with players. Almost everything I've tried to do over the last fifteen years has sought to help the not-so-religious gain a clearer picture of the 'brand' of faith that has convinced me.

Although my topic is much broader in this book – five major faiths instead of just one – the same thing motivates me: I want to help the average person on the street to explore the big questions in a non-threatening way. There is no religious 'sell' here. It is not even a minor purpose of this book to criticize the different world Faiths. As will soon become clear, my aims are far simpler. I hope to encourage understanding, tolerance and appreciation of the five great world religions. I also hope to expose a couple of the 'chardonnay' myths about religion that have become popular in secular society.

So take a seat on your comfy mental lounge and join me as a spectator as we sample the feast of ideas found in the world's great religions.

A Word or Two to Spectators

1 So you're going to write a book on religion!

How can someone possibly write a book on world religions when he is already a devoted follower of just one of them? This is a question I've grappled with from the very beginning of this project. The book itself, I guess, will prove whether or not I've managed to resolve it.

The dilemma is made more complicated because of my particular education. At first glance, being a student of both 'theology' and 'history' might seem like the perfect background for someone trying to discuss the spiritual traditions of the centuries. Yes and no.

The problem with theology and history

Theology can at times be overly theoretical in its discussion of religious issues. As the 'study of the divine', theology tends to focus on doctrines and philosophy and can sometimes leave aside the equally important issues of a religion's place in history, or (perhaps more importantly) its significance in the lives of those who practise it.

There's a danger in being a *Christian* theologian in particular. We are tempted to ask the wrong questions about other religions. Asking, for example, 'What does Buddhism teach about sin?' might be interesting to the average church 'punter' but it doesn't help the many 'spectators' out there to appreciate what Buddhism is really about. Buddha didn't have much to say about 'sin'.

Being a student of 'history' has its own peculiarities, and if these aren't kept in check they can easily make the historian irrelevant in the quest to understand religion. Historians pride themselves on being 'critical' in the study of history. But, when it comes to spiritual things, this is not always a good thing. Lengthy discussions about whether the Christian Gospels were written after the Roman invasion of Jerusalem (AD 70) or before, or whether Muhammad died prior to the battle for Palestine or after, or whether Israel's exodus from Egypt occurred in the thirteenth century BC or the fifteenth century BC, do not enhance our understanding of what it's like to be a Christian, Muslim or Jew at all. And yet historians love talking about this stuff. The historical emphasis can obscure the very obvious 'personal' dimensions of religious faith.

The importance of theology and history

Before you close this book and try to find one written by someone who is *not* into theology and history, let me suggest why these tags ('theologian', 'historian', as well as 'Christian') might not be completely useless labels to wear when writing a book on world religions.

To begin with, most religions *do* have a bit to say about God, creation, salvation and philosophical questions. So a *theological* perspective is crucial for getting inside the head of a religious faith. By contrast, recently I read a book about Islam that gave lots of names and dates but very little about the things that really make Muslims tick – things like 'God' and God's 'will for our lives'. Theology counts, and this book will hopefully show why.

The historical perspective can also prove helpful as long as we don't get carried away with it. Religions *are* historical things, that's for sure. Each of them developed at a certain point in time and as a result of particular cultural forces. Understanding these historical influences can help us appreciate more fully what was distinctive about a particular religion and what early believers found attractive about it. To give just one example, it was not until I realized that first-century Palestine had laws against mixing with 'unreligious' and 'immoral' people that I appreciated how outrageous was Jesus' habit of going to parties with prostitutes and crooked businessmen. But more about that later. My point is: without getting technical, throughout this book I hope to point out interesting connections between religion and historical background.

The problem of bias

But what about the *Christian* tag I'm wearing: is it possible for a believer in Christ to write about, say, Judaism, without letting his bias get in the way? Don't I think the Jews killed Jesus? Won't that colour the way I present the Jewish faith? Strictly speaking it was the Romans who killed Jesus but, leaving that aside, let me explain why being committed to Christianity should actually provide a *safeguard* against bias in the presentation of other people's religions.

Firstly, someone who believes in a personal God cannot write a book like this without the distinct feeling that the Almighty is looking over the shoulder. The effect of this on how honestly you describe the beliefs of others is very real, let me assure you. Of course, I'm not saying Christians are above lying or stretching the truth – they are not – but I am saying that knowing Someone Up There cares about how faithfully I portray the opinions of others weighs heavily on my mind as a writer. Any faults in my portrayal of other religions arise, I trust, not from my bias but from more general deficiencies.

There is a second, 'theological' reason my belief in Christianity *ought* to lead away from bias. It has to do with spiritual confidence. It may seem at first that the more confident you are in a particular religion the more likely you are to 'fudge' your description of another religion. Actually, I think the reverse is true. Bias in the description of other Faiths is a sure sign of a *lack* of confidence in one's own Faith. I can't speak for other Christian writers, but it seems to me perfectly obvious that if someone feels the need to misrepresent, say, Islam, in order to make Christianity look good, that person's Christian belief is anything but confident.

If Christianity is uniquely true, its beauty will be best seen only when viewed amidst a full and fair account of the alternatives. Let me give you an analogy that comes to mind. Imagine yourself as an art curator who is convinced that one piece in his collection has an unequalled quality. What will you do? Will you dim the lights on the 'competitors' in the gallery and put the spotlights on your favourite piece? Of course not. That would be a sure sign you were not actually convinced about the special beauty of your treasured masterpiece. I mean, if you've got to obscure the other pieces in order to make your favourite one look good, something is clearly wrong. A truly assured curator, that is, one with a deep confidence in the excellence of his prized item, would place all the gallery lights on full, confident that as careful art-lovers inspect the whole collection, viewing all the works in their best light, one painting, in particular, will draw people's attention.

This is a little how I felt as I wrote this book. I am more than ever convinced that each of the world's religions is a 'work of art', worthy of a public showing in the best light. At the same time, I am also more than ever confident of the unique character of the Christian faith. I can think of no better way to help readers see that quality than to turn all the gallery lights on full and let you view the whole collection for yourself.

In the next chapter I want to offer a few tips on how to get the most out of a book on world religions.

2 Tips for reading the religions

As the title makes clear, this book is not written for religious devotees but for spectators, those with a simple curiosity about Hinduism, Buddhism, Judaism, Christianity and Islam.

In our multicultural society such curiosity is a worthy thing. I enjoy the culinary benefits of multiculturalism – *Pad Thai* is my favourite dish. But with this enjoyment comes a certain obligation, I believe, to understand a little about how our new neighbours view the world. Nothing provides a better window into a culture's views than its religion. When you sit in your local Thai restaurant, wouldn't it be nice to know why there is a little shrine on the wall? This is not simply a decoration. Nor is it there to appear 'authentically Asian'. If you happen to ask, you'll probably find that the shrine represents an important part of your Buddhist restauranteur's life. If nothing else, by the end of this book you will be able to eat out at your local Indian, Thai, Chinese, Persian and Kosher restaurants and explain to your friends what makes Buddhism different from Hinduism, and how Islam responded to the Jewish and Christian communities of its time. Hopefully, there will be some additional spin-offs as well.

The importance of the world religions

Of course, religion is far more than a topic of dinner party conversation. It is fair to say that nothing has influenced the world – for good and ill – more than the world religions. Much of the world's art and music grew out of religious devotion. Music historians will often tell you how rock grew out of gospel, and how classical grew out of medieval church music.

The social laws of most societies were shaped decisively by religion. In recent times, academic ethicists have sought to distance morality from religion, insisting that one doesn't need a big spiritual truth in order to find a solid intellectual basis for ethical living – that's a debate for another book. However, there's no denying the simple social observation that throughout the history of the world religion has played a large part in organizing our views of right and wrong.

The big questions addressed by the world religions are truly universal: Who are we? What is our worth? How should we live? Are we alone? Because of this, I've often described the religious inclinations of humanity as *common sense*. My atheist friends don't like this very much but I think it is nonetheless true. The human fascination with religion is like the human interest in music, art and learning. They are found all throughout the world. They are, if you like, among the few universally shared pursuits of *Homo sapiens* throughout time. I can't speak authoritatively for art or music, but in the case of religion it is no exaggeration to say that every single society about which anthropologists and historians know anything significant has made religion a central part of its cultural life. In this way, religious questions are common sense – they are 'common' to our humanity.

I want now to offer a few tips about how to get the most out of our exploration of the world religions. Some of the suggestions will be immediately obvious; others may only appear valid as you progress through the book.

Tip one: assume nothing

When studying religion, I have found it helpful – even if only as an experiment – to assume nothing about what the various Faiths teach. Of course, we all have a vague idea of what they're on about: Jews avoid pork; Buddhists burn incense, and Muslims say prayers. But sometimes these 'obvious' expressions of faith tell you very little about what the religion really teaches. In fact, they can even give entirely the wrong impression. Buddha would roll in his grave if he heard me say Buddhism has 'something to do with burning incense'.

Making assumptions about other religions can have the effect of lowering our tolerance for difficult concepts. When faced with an idea that appears a little complex – say, the central Buddhist belief that the human 'self' does not exist – we may well give up trying to understand it, and revert to our easier, perhaps simplistic, ideas about what the religion teaches: 'Oh, Buddhism is all about tranquility and world peace.'

So, unless you happen to be an expert in comparative religion – in which case, assume away – try to suspend all assumptions and preconceptions about religion as you make your way through this book. From experience, I think you might be surprised by the result.

Tip two: throw out the 'categories'

In some books and courses on world religions authors try to fit the teachings of the various Faiths into categories which are thought to be common to all world religions.

I've come across two forms of this approach. The first is found in *Christian* books about world religions. When I first became interested in world religions, ten or so years ago, I read numerous books about Buddhism, Islam, and so on, all written *by* Christians, *for* Christians, and from the *Christian perspective* (I was an eager frequenter of Christian bookshops in those days). Such books tend to describe non-Christian religions using the mental categories of Christianity. Because Christianity has a lot to say about sin, forgiveness and eternal life, these books set out to analyze religions on the basis of these topics. Christian categories are imposed on non-Christian faiths. The authors asked questions such as: What does Buddhism teach about sin? How do Hindus understand forgiveness? What does a Jew do to receive eternal life? and so on.

This approach certainly succeeds in helping Christians feel better about their particular views on sin, forgiveness and eternal life, but it does not help readers understand the world religions on their own terms and in their own categories. I've often wondered what it would look like if an author set out to describe Christianity from the perspective of the Buddhist concepts of 'Self', *karma* and rebirth. I imagine Christianity would look rather thin.

My point is: approaching the world religions *on their own terms* is the only way really to understand them. For my fellow Christian readers, I would add that this is also the only way to engage in meaningful conversation about Christ with those from other religions.

There is also a non-religious version of the attempt to fit all religions into pre-determined categories. And it too can obscure rather than clarify. One influential textbook I read recently describes the world Faiths using the same six categories: sacred narrative, doctrine, ritual, institutional expression, experience and ethics.

The categories are sometimes helpful. Most of the religions do have something to say about 'ethics', for instance. The problem is: presenting the Faiths in these neat categories leaves the impression that the great world religions are all asking exactly the same questions – but just arriving at different answers.

The reality is quite different. To give just one example, Hinduism has very little to say in the category of 'institutional expression'. It rarely asks: how are worshippers to be led and organized? There are no Hindu 'bishops', head offices, official councils, or even anything resembling a church (Hindu temples serve a different function). Compared with, say, Christianity, Hinduism is virtually institution-less. But if I provided a chapter on Christianity's institutional expression followed by one on Hinduism's institutional expression this would obscure the relative emphases of the two religions. Readers would be left with the rather false impression that these Faiths are simply arriving at different answers to the same questions.

Imagine if I were to set out to write a book on five world sports – soccer, rugby, racing, Judo and synchronized swimming – and tried to explain these codes using a set of predetermined categories: let's say, scoring, speed, force, training, playing field, and so on. I may be able to squeeze all the sports into these categories. But would this help readers understand each sport from its own perspective? I doubt it. The categories would help the look of my Contents page: 'The Use of Force in Judo'; 'The Use of Force in Synchronized Swimming', and so on. But they probably would not help readers appreciate what it's like to perform a *Tomoe Nagi* on an opponent, or to execute a synchronized leg-lift with twirl (I can't say I've performed both of these). The concepts of 'force', 'scoring', and so on, mean totally different things in each case. The various sports, you could say, are asking different questions.

You will notice as you read on that very few of the same terms make an appearance across the chapters, except where these terms are explicitly shared by the religions themselves. This may prove frustrating at times, since our natural tendency is to want to organize disparate ideas into coherent concepts. But it is my firm belief that to understand the world religions we must resist the temptation to file their various teachings into predetermined categories.

Tip three: allow the differences

I was once asked at a dinner party about the similarities between the religions. It had come up in conversation that I was writing a book on the topic, and this rather sophisticated middle-aged gentleman, with white wine in hand, piped up: 'Tell me, if one were to set out the teachings of the various religions in a paradigm, where might I see some white spaces?' I had no idea what he meant, so he kindly rephrased: 'If one set out the beliefs of the world religions in a kind of spreadsheet grid and shaded in those boxes where their teachings overlapped, would there be any un-shaded areas?' In other words, he was asking if all the religions basically teach the same thing. I surprised him by replying, perhaps a little provocatively, 'There would be far more un-shaded boxes than shaded ones – not much overlap at all!'

As it turns out, this gentleman's wife was due to attend a day-long course on world religions the very next weekend. She was hoping, she explained to me, to discover what all the great Faiths had in common. I think I disappointed her. The topic of conversation changed very quickly.

It was perhaps a little mischievous of me to say that the imagined 'religious spreadsheet' would be *mostly* white spaces, but it is not very far from the truth. One of the real keys to understanding the world religions, I believe, is to allow them to have their differences.

It is very popular today to emphasize the sameness of the great Faiths. This is partly motivated by a desire to get along and to connect to each other as fellow members of the human family. It is also partly motivated by ignorance of the blissful kind. At a great distance most people look pretty much the same. Close up, however, it's a different story. Along similar lines, I find it humorous whenever I hear people from Asia say that Westerners 'all look the same' (there is also a reverse Western-Asian claim, of course). It reminds me that if you never mix with people from different races you will have no eye for detail. The same is true with religion. The statement, 'All religions are basically the same', is born of the same lack of acquaintance as 'All Asians look the same.'

At a distance, it probably does seem as though Hinduism, Buddhism, Judaism, Christianity and Islam teach many of the same things. They all have beautiful buildings of worship, they all teach that we should be nice to people, and they all offer prayers to a divinity (well, almost all of them do). When one begins to look more closely, however, it becomes clear that the religions are only *superficially* similar. They are substantially different.

One reason for the dissimilarity of some of the religions is that they emerged in cultures utterly different from one another (Hinduism and Judaism, for example). They are different people in different times asking different questions about different things.

Another reason for religious differences is that some of the world Faiths arose as deliberate critiques of what came before. Take Hinduism and Buddhism. A large part of the Buddha's teaching was designed to challenge the Hinduism of his day.

Who am I all these years later to say that the differences don't really matter?

Instead of trying to harmonize, say, the Buddhist and Hindu concepts of the 'soul', I should try to follow the arguments of each and learn to appreciate the differing conclusions. That is certainly what Buddha and the Hindu gurus would have asked of us.

By seeking to affirm the sameness of the world religions, modern societies like ours are in danger of honouring none of them. For if we squash distinctions between them and quash debate about them we are not really listening to them. As unpopular as the idea appears to have become, we simply must allow the world religions to have their distinct voices and to express their (often very) different points of view.

Why the 'big five'?

You've probably worked out already that I intend to focus on just five religions: Hinduism, Buddhism, Judaism, Christianity and Islam. The rationale for including four of these is simple. Numerically, they are the largest world religions: in descending order, Christianity, Islam, Hinduism and Buddhism. The fifth largest religion is actually Sikhism.

So why include Judaism (the sixth largest religion) over Sikhism? Firstly, despite its relative small numbers, Judaism is found in 134 countries worldwide, making it more 'international' than Sikhism (34 countries), Buddhism (129 countries) and Hinduism (114 countries). Christianity, by the way, is found in 238 countries and Islam in 206 (*Britannica Book of the Year 2004*).

The second reason is perhaps a little more subjective. The words 'Israel' and 'Jew' feature almost every day on our TV screens, as we hear of peace deals, increased tensions and bloodshed. A deeper knowledge of the Jewish worldview (along with that of Islam) is, I think, a necessity of the times.

A third reason for including Judaism is its significance for the two largest world religions. Islam and (especially)

Christianity grew out of Jewish belief. The faith of Israel, in other words, has influenced the religious landscape of the world out of all proportion to its numerical size.

So, with humble apologies to my Sikh readers (who fortunately believe in showing mercy), let's begin this spectator's guide to world religions with an account of the oldest of the great Faiths.

Part 2

Hinduism
The Way of
Release

In a nutshell

Hinduism is a terrifically diverse way of life which has
thrived throughout India (mainly) for millennia. At
its heart, Hinduism teaches the wisdom and duties
necessary to be released from the cycle of life-death-
rebirth so that one's true self may return to *Brahman*,
the ultimate source of life.

3 Origins of the 'eternal religion'

When someone mentions the word '*Christ*ianity' you know immediately it has something to do with a person known as 'Christ'. When we say '*Buddh*ism' we think of that happy round fellow in the famous Asian statues (actually, Buddha was probably not 'round' at all, but don't worry about that yet).

When we come to 'Hinduism', however, things are not so simple. The name tells you absolutely nothing about the content. There was no such person as 'Hindu' and, to complicate things further, no one in India actually calls Hinduism 'Hinduism'. It's bizarre to think that the average Hindu (there are about 750 million of them, by the way) living in, say, rural Uttar Pradesh has probably never heard of something called 'Hinduism'.

The term 'Hinduism' came into Western usage via British writers in India in the 1800s who couldn't think of an appropriate term to describe the array of spiritual beliefs and practices they saw around them. To get technical for a moment: the word 'Hindu' comes from the name of the great '*Indus* River', which runs along the entire north-west borders of India (the word 'India' also comes from Indus). Calling Hinduism 'Hinduism', then, is about as helpful as calling Indigenous Australian beliefs 'Murrumbidgeeism' (after the Murrumbidgee River)!

The fact that these nineteenth-century writers couldn't come up with a better name for Indian religion actually illustrates something very important about the topic of this chapter: 'Hinduism' is not one neat, easily understood religious system. More than any other tradition discussed in this book, Hinduism is a large cocktail of rituals, beliefs, practices and exercises ('yoga', remember!) with no historical founder and no institutional hierarchy – there's no Pope or Dalai Lama in this religion.

'Cocktail' is not a flippant description because the official religion of India can be compared (hopefully without any offence to Hindus) to an enormous party full of colours, music, food and dancing. Some at the party are loud and boisterous; others are deep in conversation. Still others are sitting by themselves gazing into nothingness – and they're quite happy about it too.

For simplicity's sake we're going to use the word 'Hinduism' throughout this book, but please keep in mind that the collection of traditions described here is just that – a 'collection', a fascinating, daring, and (for some Westerners) bewildering assortment of ideas and activities.

So where did it all begin?

The oldest religion in the world?

What is called 'Hinduism' in the West is known as *sanatana dharma* in India. These words, which come from ancient Sanskrit, mean 'eternal law/religion'. Whether or not the religion is literally *eternal* is for others to judge. One thing is certain, though: Hinduism is very, very old. In fact, scholars usually identify Hinduism as the oldest of the world religions. Jewish people might have a problem with this description since the 'big guns' of the Jewish Scriptures – Joseph (1700s BC), Abraham (1800s BC), and Noah (well, who knows?) – are very ancient. Nevertheless, it is conventional to think of 'Judaism' in the official sense as beginning with Moses (of 'Ten Commandments' fame) sometime in the mid- to late 1200s BC.

Hinduism pips Judaism at the post, then, by just a few hundred years. The story of Indian religion begins around 1500 BC, when the nomadic Aryan tribes (originally from Persia) settled in India, bringing their religion with them. This Aryan religion is known as 'Vedism' and it was the basis, or first layer at least, of what we would eventually call Hinduism.

From the Vedism of these early settlers to the full-blown religion of Hinduism there was a long history of reflection and development. The best way to appreciate this development is to think of Hinduism as being made up of three layers (or ingredients in a cocktail). These layers correspond to three slightly overlapping periods in Indian history, each with its own set of sacred writings: the *Vedas* (1500–500 BC), the *Upanishads* (1000–300 BC) and the *Smriti* writings (500 BC–AD 300). Don't worry about these names and dates right now but just remember that, taken together, these three interlocking traditions constitute India's 'eternal religion'.

So let's begin with the *Vedas*, the first ingredient in the cocktail that is Hinduism.

4 Gods, drugs and sacrifice: the Vedas

The word *veda* means something like 'wisdom' of the sacred kind. Because of this, the term *Vedas* (with a capital 'V') is often used to refer to *all* of the Hindu Scriptures, a little like the way Christians talk about the 'Bible'.

But there is a stricter meaning of the term *Vedas*. Many Hindus use the word to refer only to the earliest writings of Hinduism, those composed between 1500 and 500 BC and reflecting the original *Vedic* religion of the Aryan settlers mentioned in the last chapter. This is the way I'll use the word throughout this chapter. The later writings, which we'll look at in a moment, have their own important names and categorization.

There are four basic *Vedas* (in this strict sense), which in published form would fill a bookshelf:

1. *Wisdom of Verses (Rig-veda)*. This is a collection of about 1,000 hymns that were sung in connection with ancient rituals designed to keep the gods in favour. Animal sacrifices, fire offerings, as well as the drinking of hallucinogenic plant juice, were all part of the highly complex 'liturgy' (or act of worship) described here.

2. *Wisdom of the Sacrificial Formulas (Yajur-veda)*. This contains the words that were to be said by a priest as these rituals took place. The words often involved praise of the gods.

3. *Wisdom of the Chants (Sama-veda)*. This mainly contains verses from the first *Veda (Rig-veda)* but with indications of how they are to be chanted with fixed melodies.

4. *Wisdom of the Atharvan Priests (Atharva-veda)*. This is a little bit different from (and was probably written later than) the first three. It is a collection of hymns, prayers and curses of a more 'magical' nature.

Attached to these four *Vedas* are various discussions, explanations and amplifications of the rituals. These extensions are known as the *Brahmanas*, *Aranyakas* and *Upanishads*, and were written later than the original collections. These extensions mark a clear development in the outlook of the early *Vedic* material. This is particularly the case in the *Upanishads*, which will be discussed in the next section.

For now we should ask: what aspects of Hinduism are revealed in this first layer, the *Vedas*? Two ideas deserve mention.

Lots of gods

One of the most obvious aspects of the religion of the *Vedas* is a belief in a great variety of gods. The technical word for this is 'polytheism' (Greek for 'many gods'). In contrast to religions such as Judaism and Islam, which insist there is just one God, the world of the *Vedas* is one full of powerful, unpredictable beings – usually called *'devas'*.

There are about 1,000 *devas* mentioned in the *Vedas*. Some of them are decent, some are evil, and all of them deserve the respect of human beings. The main gods of early Hindu polytheism include Indra, the warrior and storm god, Agni, the god of fire, and Soma, the god associated with the plant juice the priest drinks in one of the main *Vedic* rituals. Other gods such as Vishnu and Siva (also spelt Shiva) make minor appearances in the *Vedas* but will later come to dominate the religious landscape.

For now it is just worth noticing that Indian religion began with a belief in many gods, each with its own role to play in the cosmos. This feature still exists in modern Hinduism but in a slightly different way, as we shall see later.

Rituals and sacrifice

Two rituals were important in the ancient *Vedas*. The first was that of the *Soma*. This involved a priest taking the juice of a (now unknown) plant and pouring it over an altar. The priest also drank some of the drug and literally got high. The intoxicating effect of the juice was thought to be divine and so was able to communicate special powers and favours to the worshippers:

> *I have tasted the sweet drink of life, knowing that it inspires good thoughts and joyous expansiveness to the extreme, that all the gods and mortals seek it together, calling it honey. When you penetrate inside, you will know no limits, and you will avert the wrath of the gods... Let the drops protect me from the foot that stumbles and keep lameness away from me. Inflame me like a fire kindled by friction; make us see far; make us richer, better. For when I am intoxicated with you, Soma, I think myself rich. Draw near and make us thrive* (Wisdom of the Verses, *or* Rig-veda 8:48.1–15).

The second important ritual in the *Vedas* is the fire ritual. Here a priest places an animal on the altar and sets it alight. The fire is considered to be the manifestation of Agni (the fire god), who consumes the sacrifice on behalf of the other gods. When the sacrifice is accepted by the god (burnt up by the flames) the blessings of the gods will be granted to the worshippers. To this day in India, many upper-class families (or *Brahmans*) maintain a small household fire in honour of the god Agni. It is amazing to think that a custom that started three and half thousand years ago is still practised today.

Other rituals from the *Vedas* that still exist in Hinduism today include the Indian wedding ceremony (the oldest in the world) and the common Hindu practice of ceremonially cremating the dead. Temple worship and offerings, reminiscent of the ancient *Vedic* rituals, still feature prominently in Indian religious life.

Indian religion developed out of the *Vedas*, and belief in these writings is still a basic tenet of Hinduism. However, Hinduism did not limit itself to the ideas found in these ancient Scriptures. Some of the most important themes of Hinduism were still to come. These emerged not out of the *Vedic* material but out of what Hindus call the *Vedanta*, or 'conclusion of the *Vedas*', a term used to describe another set of written traditions known as the *Upanishads*.

5 God, the soul and entrapment: the Upanishads

The term *Upanishad* literally means 'sitting near'. It is an allusion to sitting in a class, learning from the great teachers of India. And that is exactly what these writings are about. In the period after the writing of the early *Vedas* many Indian gurus began to reflect deeply on the content of their religion and sought to make sense of the world in light of that tradition. What these gurus came up with is recorded in the twelve classical *Upanishads* (composed between 1000 and 300 BC). These are regarded by many as the real sacred writings of Hinduism. Certainly in terms of their theoretical contribution to Hinduism the *Upanishads* far outweigh the *Vedas*.

The *Upanishads* contain parables and anecdotes, dense philosophical argumentation, dialogues, poems and proverbs. Behind it all, however, stands the claim that reading this material (and, of course, understanding it) will give you ultimate insight into life, the universe and everything. I cannot promise you that much, but I can point you in the direction of four of the most important beliefs to crystallize in the great *Upanishads*.

Brahman: the One behind the many
Already in the *Wisdom of the Verses*, the oldest of the Hindu writings, reference is made to a mysterious background force in the universe known as *Brahman*. Think perhaps of the

'Force' in the *Star Wars* movies. Little is made of *brahman* in these early Scriptures except that the priest who conducts the rituals is himself called a *brahman*. The idea here is that the priest is connected to the life force of the universe. He is therefore able to harness its power for the sake of the worshippers.

In the *Upanishads*, *brahman* experiences something of a magnification. From the status of a cosmic 'background' power, *Brahman* (now it needs a capital 'B') is elevated to the level of the Ultimate and Only reality in the universe. From *Brahman* everything in the universe came; to *Brahman* everything in the universe will return.

Brahman is a difficult concept to grasp for people brought up in the Western world. Westerners can cope with the idea of a physical universe, and they can cope with the concept of a universal God. But when these two concepts are brought together into one mega-idea, we begin to scratch our heads. In India, however, the idea of the ONE (*Brahman*) is a key aspect of a person's upbringing. It is part of the way they look at the world. The philosophical name for this fundamental Hindu idea is 'pantheism', from the Greek for *everything is God*.

The analogy of a fire might help. A fire produces sparks which flit about for a while and then disappear. Often they disappear back into the flame from which they came. There is a sense in which the spark and the flame are both separate and not separate. They are separate in that the spark is visible independently of the flame, but they are not separate in as much as the spark came from the flame, is made of the same stuff, and ultimately returns to the flame, where it is absorbed back into its source. This is something like how Hinduism understands the universe. *Brahman* is the flame from which everything originates – creation, humans, the gods, and so on. All these things flicker for a while and then return to their source, where they are absorbed into the Ultimate and only true reality.

Is *Brahman* 'God' in the Western sense of that word? It comes close. The problem is: it is unclear in the texts of the *Upanishads* whether or not we are to think of *Brahman* as a conscious and personal being. Most Hindus do believe in personal gods. However, they do so not with *Brahman* in mind but by concentrating on one of *Brahman*'s emanations, such as Vishnu or Siva. According to the teaching of the *Upanishads*, these more personal deities are themselves 'sparks' from the ultimately unfathomable Flame that is *Brahman*. It should be noted that some contemporary Indians choose to believe in the existence of a single God and regard the emanations of that God (Vishnu, etc.) as metaphors of the divine character.

Atman: the soul and the Soul

Connected with the idea of *Brahman* is the concept of the *atman*, or soul. This is the 'inner-you', the real, eternal life-force that exists in every living creature.

The *Upanishads* teach that this real you – as opposed to your mere physical and psychological characteristics – is a reflection of the ultimate force, *Brahman*. It is a 'spark' from the big Flame.

The Hindu concept of the *atman* mustn't be confused with Western ideas about the human soul or spirit which is thought to go to heaven when we die. *Atman* is more a life-principle that animates your existence. It is the eternal YOU that lies behind your everyday consciousness. If you think this sounds vaguely like the concept of *Brahman*, you are right. The *atman* is that part of you that is from *Brahman*.

It is very important that we get our heads around the idea that this real you (the *atman*) corresponds to the ultimate reality behind the universe (or *Brahman*). Understanding this provides the basis for understanding the Hindu concepts of 'entrapment' and 'liberation'. In Hinduism, the goal of life is to free the *atman* (the real you) from the impurities of worldly existence so that it might return to *Brahman*, as a spark returns to its flame. First we'll talk about the 'trap' we are all in, according to Hinduism, then we'll look at how to escape.

Samsara: entrapment in an endless cycle

In Western cultures, 'reincarnation' (bodily re-existence in this world after death) is often thought of as an exciting experience: 'I was an Amazon Queen in a former life'; 'I hope I come back as an eagle.' From the point of view of Hinduism, statements like these involve a basic misunderstanding of the important idea of *samsara* ('the running around'). *Samsara* refers to the potentially endless snare of being born in this physical world, dying and then having to be reborn again. It is a snare that catches all living beings, even insects. It is an 'entrapment'.

The *Upanishads* describe this cycle of birth-death-and-rebirth not as an opportunity to 'come back and have another go' but as a regurgitation into the harsh realities of physical existence. At best this existence is fleeting and false; at worst, it is evil and impure. The realities of earthly existence (and re-existence) are described by the gurus of the *Upanishads* as a foul stench unpleasantly attaching themselves to your true soul (your *atman*), which is trapped in this physical world.

At this point you may be thinking: 'But I like my life: it's rich, fun, and full of friendship and things to learn.' The teachers of the *Upanishads* would regard such thinking as short-sighted and ultimately tragic. Why would a little 'spark' want to remain a spark when it could return to the great flame from which it had come? Why would it not want to experience the fullness of its own true nature by merging with its source?

So what is the cause of this entrapment in the cycle of birth, death and rebirth? What is it that makes the 'stench' fix itself upon our soul, preventing us from returning to the purity of our Source, *Brahman*? Answer: *karma*.

Karma: the power behind entrapment

The concept of being 'trapped' is better understood when we look at the connected idea of *karma*. Literally, this word means 'action' but it includes the idea of the consequences of action as well. *Karma* is sometimes translated in the Hindu Scriptures (in English) as 'fruititive action' – action which bears fruit.

Karma is one of those well-used words in Western society: people experience a bit of bad luck and sometimes say, 'Oh, bad *karma*'; they may witness someone doing a 'good deed' and declare, 'Good *karma* for you, pal!'

This popular understanding of *karma* is actually not too far off the mark. In short, the Hindu teaching about *karma* (Buddhism has its own version) insists that all of your actions in life 'attach' themselves to you. They stick to your Soul in such a way as to determine your Soul's re-existence, your next 'incarnation'.

> *According as one acts, according as one conducts himself, so does he become. The doer of good becomes good. The doer of evil becomes evil. One becomes virtuous by virtuous action, bad by bad action... As is his desire, such is his resolve; as is his resolve, such is the action he performs; what action (karma) he performs, that he procures for himself... Where one's mind is attached – the inner self goes thereto with action, being attached to it alone. Obtaining the end of his action, whatever he does in this world, he comes again from that world to this world of action* (Brhadaranyaka Upanishad).

You may have heard people joke about someone deserving to come back as a 'cockroach': in orthodox Hinduism this is a real possibility.

To understand all these ideas properly we have to realize that coming back as something a little bit better in the next life (let's say a wealthy rock star or a beautiful princess) is not, strictly speaking, a good thing. It is simply the lesser of two evils. The ultimate goal for the Hindu is not to come back as something better next time around; it is to escape the need to come back at all. According to the teaching of the *Upanishads*, even wealthy rock stars and princesses (not that these were actually discussed by the great gurus) are trapped in the unreality of existence. The rich and famous, just like the rest of us, are unable to feel the warmth, or see the light, of the ultimate flame of *Brahman*. Something better than 'good *karma*' is needed for true liberation.

Moksha: release into ultimate reality

Well, if *karma* and 'entrapment' are the bad news of Hinduism, what's the good news? The answer lies in another important teaching of the *Upanishads*, the idea of *moksha*.

Once we understand the concepts of *karma* and entrapment the idea of *moksha* doesn't require much explanation. *Moksha* is simply 'release' from the futile cycle of re-existence (caused by *karma*), so that you can enter into the reality of *Brahman*, the Source of true existence. As the *Svetasvatara Upanishad* says: *Brahman*-knowers become merged in *Brahman*, intent thereon, liberated from the womb (i.e., from rebirth).

This liberation is likened in the *Upanishads* to a snake shedding its skin, a drop of water falling into the ocean and, as I've already said, a spark returning to its flame. Your previously trapped soul is reabsorbed into the ultimate reality of *Brahman*.

Is this release like heaven, then? Well, not really. Usually, when people speak about heaven (and we'll have more to say about that later), they mean a place where individuals consciously enjoy each other and God. This is not what Hinduism envisages when it speaks of release from entrapment. In fact, according to Hinduism, the notion of individual personality is part of your ignorant separation from *Brahman*. Release, or *moksha*, involves the merging of your Soul back into the Ultimate Soul.

Will you be *conscious* in this experience of release? Hinduism gives different answers to this question, and it depends on what you mean by 'you' and 'conscious'. It is probably true to say that the you reading this book will not be individually conscious when absorbed into *Brahman*. However, since *Brahman* is 'pure consciousness', being absorbed into that reality will be more about gaining true consciousness (*Brahman*'s consciousness) than losing your current consciousness. A spark returning to the flame may lose its individual shape, colour and warmth but it gains the greater shape, colour and warmth of the Flame. The Hindu concept of release (*moksha*) is somewhat similar.

How can we experience this *moksha*? What is the path to liberation? That is the subject of our next chapter.

6 Caste, duty and salvation: the Smriti literature

So far we have been discussing ideas that emerge in the earliest and most authoritative writings of Hinduism, the *Vedas* and the *Upanishads*. These make up the first two layers of Hindu tradition. Hindus call this material *scruti*, which literally means 'heard'. It is a reference to the belief that these teachings have existed from eternity and were simply 'heard' by certain gurus who passed them on.

As a Trivial Pursuit™ aside, Hindus believe that the universe appears and disappears every 24 million years (12 million years of existence followed by 12 million years of non-existence). According to Hindus, the *Vedas* (along with the *Upanishads*) are revealed to human teachers at the beginning of each new cosmic cycle.

'Remembered' writings

The final scriptures to be discussed in this chapter are known as the *smriti*, or 'remembered' writings. Although regarded as less *authoritative* than the 'heard' scriptures, this 'remembered' literature is every bit as popular as the *Vedas*. Many would say even more so. These texts have had an enormous influence on the beliefs and practices of modern Hindus.

Most important among these 'remembered' writings are two great epic poems known as the *Romance of Rama* (the *Ramayana*), written some time after 300 BC, and the *Great Epic of the Bharata Dynasty* (*Mahabharata*), composed a century or more later.

The *Romance of Rama* is, of course, a 'romance'. It is a big love story about Rama, a royal and divine figure, and his wife, Princess Sita. Throughout the narrative there are contests with the gods, accusations of adultery, kidnapping (of Sita) by demons, and a daring rescue conducted by Rama and a warrior-monkey named Hanuman (I'd love to see this on the big screen). On the basis of this narrative, many in India still worship Rama as the god of virtue and chivalry. Hanuman, the monkey god, is also worshipped in India today, and monkeys (living ones) are widely regarded as sacred.

The Bhagavad-gita, or Song of the Lord

Of more interest for understanding the key beliefs of Hinduism is the *Great Epic of the Bharata Dynasty* (*Mahabharata*). At the centre of this massive mythological epic is a battle between cousins, after which almost the entire race is destroyed. Just before the bloody battle an extraordinary conversation breaks out between the hero of the story, Prince Arjuna, and his advisor Krishna, who turns out to be an incarnation of the god Vishnu.

The poetic account of this conversation runs to about seventy pages in my copy and forms what is known as the *Bhagavad-gita* (the *Song of the Lord*). This is a text regarded by many as the most treasured portion of all the Hindu Scriptures. It is certainly the most widely published. For this reason, it is important to talk a little more about the *Bhagavad-gita* and what it teaches.

Just before Prince Arjuna gets ready to slay the opposing armies he pauses for a moment and begins to wonder whether he should not in fact lay down his weapons and avoid shedding blood. Enter: the divine Krishna, the Prince's charioteer, who reveals to Arjuna the wisdom he needs to fulfil his duty. Taking Krishna's advice, Arjuna launches into battle and emerges the winner.

Don't think for a moment that the *Bhagavad-gita* is simply a text justifying warfare. Most Hindus reject the way of violence. The purpose of this popular part of the Hindu Scriptures is religious more than political. In the next few pages we shall see just how much the *Bhagavad-gita* has influenced modern Hinduism.

The four 'castes' of people

One of the important themes in the *Bhagavad-gita* is a concept that sounds quite foreign to egalitarian societies such as that Australia aspires to be. Here is one of those moments when understanding another person's point of view requires humility and open-mindedness.

As early as the first *Vedas*, the Hindu Scriptures talked about human society (Indian at least) in four categories, or castes. In the *Bhagavad-gita* the god Krishna endorses this hierarchical view of humanity in an important way.

The four *varnas*, or 'castes', of people are as follows:

1. Priests (*Brahmans*). *Brahmans* are regarded as the descendants of the original *Vedic* priests (1500 BC). They form the top layer in Indian society and are considered blessed with nearness to the ultimate life-principle of the universe. Hence the name '*Brahmans*'.

2. Warrior-kings (*Ksatriya*). Also prominent in the *Vedas*, and especially prominent in the *Bhagavad-gita*, are those who make up the second layer of Indian society, the 'warrior-kings'. These are thought by Hindus to be the descendants of the original commanders of the ancient *Vedic* state. Arjuna, the princely hero of the *Bhagavad-gita*, belonged to this caste. 'Warrior-kings' in contemporary Indian society tend to occupy what we would call the 'upper-middle-class'.

3. Common people (*Vaisyas*). Still regarded as descendants of the original Aryan people, the 'common people' make up the bulk of Indian society and are meant to be occupied with industry and economy. They are the 'workers' of society, you might say.

4. Servants (*Sudras*). Hindu society regards the fourth caste of person as sharing nothing of the *Vedic* heritage. Their role is simply to serve the three upper castes of India. A 'servant' can only hope that his or her *karma* will cause a 'promotion' in the

next life. Only by being born a 'priest', 'warrior-king' or 'common person' does a person have a share in *Brahman* and a chance at release (*moksha*). If this sounds a little unfair, the Hindu Scriptures would explain that the place of the 'servant' at the bottom of Indian society is simply the outworking of his or her *karma*.

The exclusion of the 'servants' from Indian society is emphasized by the fact that only those from the three upper castes of India undergo the most important ceremony of a Hindu boy's life. The 'twice-born' ceremony (the *dvija*) is perhaps the equivalent of baptism in Christianity, or the *bar mitzvah* in Judaism. The ceremony involves placing a sacred thread (like a sash) over the left shoulder of the child (eight years old) and across his right hip. The ritual symbolizes the child taking on his duties as a member of Hindu society: this is thought of as a 'second birth'. The 'servant' caste in Indian society, however, has no opportunity in *this* life for a second birth.

It must be pointed out, however, that since the time of the great Indian activist Mahatma Gandhi (died 1948) traditional Hindu ideas about the castes have been greatly challenged. Influenced by Gandhi, many modern Indians endorse a more egalitarian view of society than that observed in these sacred writings. As a result, the popularity of the *dvija* ceremony has waned somewhat in contemporary Indian society. Some Hindus even reject the ritual as overly exclusive.

The idea of four castes, or *varnas*, is important to the *Bhagavad-gita* and provides the rationale for Krishna's instruction to Prince Arjuna that he *should* go into battle. After all, the prince belonged to the caste of 'warrior-kings': it was his place in life to work and fight for matters of state. To do otherwise would be to try to defy *karma* and reject his universally appointed duty, his *dharma*. Rejecting one's *dharma* forfeits one's hope of 'release' (*moksha*).

In the process of instructing Arjuna about his duty (*dharma*), the god Krishna explains to the prince the three paths to liberation that are available to the faithful Hindu. Here is where the *Bhagavad-gita* makes its most significant contribution to Indian religion. Faithful Hindus today hope eventually to experience 'release' by following one (or a combination) of these three *margas*, or paths.

The three paths are ways of escaping birth and rebirth and so returning to *Brahman*. Hence, each path has the name *yoga* attached to it: *yoga* means 'oneness' or 'unity' (with *Brahman*). An explanation of the three paths follows.

Path of duties (karma-yoga)

As already mentioned, Krishna explained to Prince Arjuna that it was his duty in life, his *dharma*, to fight for the interests of the state. One of the paths of salvation open to Arjuna – and to all Hindus – is to faithfully continue one's duty.

Two aspects of this duty have to be kept in mind to understand this path to liberation. First, one's *dharma* ('duty/law') is largely governed by what caste you're from. Even a so-called 'good deed', says Krishna in the *Bhagavad-gita*, is of no value if it is not a deed appropriate to your caste. Hence, although Arjuna's desire to lay down arms seemed like a nice thing to do, it was not beneficial to his liberation. Why? Because it would have been a rejection of his duty as a member of the 'warrior-king' caste. Only actions *in accordance with the duties of your caste* lead to your 'release'.

The second thing to keep in mind is that one's actions must be performed with *detachment*. That is, your actions must be done without any desire or intention for a particular outcome. This is a difficult concept, but Krishna in the *Bhagavad-gita* insists on it:

> So, without being attached to the fruits of activities, one should act as a matter of duty; for by working without attachment one attains the supreme (Bhagavad-gita 3:19).

The logic goes like this: what traps you in this world of birth and rebirth is not activity *per se* but 'fruititive activity', that is, activity done with a desire for certain outcomes. Of course, every action does have its result but only an action done with the result in mind taints your soul and traps you in this world of birth and rebirth. This is just how the universe works: it is the natural law. However, actions performed by you without attachment to particular outcomes are 'empty' actions and so attract no *karmic* effects. As a result, you can be freed from this world and so return to *Brahman*.

But what exactly are the appropriate actions of my caste that I perform as a duty with no mind to the results? To answer that question, further so-called 'remembered' writings (*smriti*) emerged in Hinduism. These are known as *dharmasutras* ('threads of duty'). The most famous of these is *The Laws of Manu* (first century BC), a book that outlines in great detail the duties of the various castes of Indian society.

Path of knowledge (jnana-yoga)

Krishna explains to Arjuna another path of salvation open to the faithful Hindu. This one had already featured prominently in the *Upanishads*. It is the Path of Knowledge.

As we've already seen, the *Upanishads* teach that your 'soul' (*atman*) is made of the same stuff, so to speak, as *Brahman*. The problem is: your soul is trapped by *karma* in the cycle of birth and rebirth (*samsara*) and is unable to merge with *Brahman*. The teachers of the *Upanishads* insisted that *contemplation* combined with rigorous self-denial could lead to the mental realization of your soul's oneness with *Brahman*. This is the Hindu ascetic path, and Krishna in the *Bhagavad-gita* endorses it, while pointing out that it is very difficult to achieve:

One should engage oneself in the practice of (jnana-) yoga with undeviating determination and faith. One should abandon, without exception, all material desires born of false ego and thus control all the senses on all sides by the mind. Gradually, step by step, with full conviction, one should become situated in trance by means of intelligence, and thus the mind should be fixed on the self alone and should think of nothing else... The yogi whose mind is fixed on me verily attains the highest happiness. By virtue *of his identity with Brahman, he is liberated; his mind is peaceful, his passions are quieted, and he is freed from sin. Steady in the self, being freed from all material contamination, the yogi achieves the highest perfectional stage of happiness in touch with the supreme consciousness (*Bhagavad-gita 6:24–28*).*

Clearly, the Path of Knowledge is radically different from the Path of Duties. Instead of trying to act with detachment, this *jnana-yoga* tries to avoid action altogether. Bodily comforts are denied, the ancient Scriptures are recited and mystical states of mind are attained (through yoga exercises and meditation). Through these practices the ascetic is able to rise above the '*karmic*-effects' that tie him to this the world, and so he merges with *Brahman* directly. He is 'released'.

Path of devotion (bhakti-yoga)

The third path to salvation is one with little precedent in the earlier writings of Hinduism. Krishna, in the *Bhagavad-gita*, reveals to Prince Arjuna a 'short-cut' (although a Hindu would not use that term) out of the trap of existence-and-re-existence and into the reality of *Brahman*. Faithful Hindus, says Krishna, can escape entrapment by *devoting* themselves utterly to one of the many gods of the Hindu pantheon, preferably to Krishna:

*Arjuna inquired: 'What's considered to be more perfect, those who are properly engaged in your devotional service, or those who worship the impersonal Brahman, the unmanifested?' The Bhagavan (Lord Krishna) said: 'He whose mind is fixed on my personal form, always engaged in worshiping me with great and supernatural faith, is considered by me to be most perfect… For one who worships me, giving up all his activities to me and being devoted to me without deviation, engaged in devotional service and always meditating on me, who has fixed his mind on me, son of Prita – for him I am the swift deliverer from the ocean of birth and death' (*Bhagavad-gita 12:1–7*).*

If you perform all your actions in this world with absolute devotion to Krishna (or some other god) he will deliver you from the effects of *karma* and you will be free.

Prince Arjuna liked the idea of the Path of Devotion. Having heard the teaching and witnessed a vision of the glory of Krishna (as an incarnation of the god Vishnu) Arjuna humbly devoted himself to Krishna.

What forms can this 'devotion' take? For some, devotion is thought of in deeply personal and emotional terms: you are to feel intense love and affection for your 'favourite god' (your *istadevata*) in all your daily affairs. For others, devotion can take a more ritualistic form: paying homage to your god in an act of temple worship such as offering food or money to the deity. Shrines are often set up in the home for this purpose.

The Path of Devotion, or *bhakti*, is probably the dominant form of Hinduism in India today, and two gods stand head and shoulders above the rest in terms of sheer numbers of devotees. These are Vishnu and Siva. From these gods derive the names of the two great 'schools' of modern Hinduism. After a brief explanation of these two traditions we can bring our exploration of Hinduism to a close.

Devotion to Vishnu (Vaishnavism)

Vaishnavism is the term used to describe the many different groups in India that are 'devoted' to the god Vishnu and his various incarnations. Worshippers tend to take what they like from the epics of his incarnations (such as the *Mahabharata* mentioned earlier) and blend these stories with local customs to produce elaborate rituals of worship.

Traditionally, Vishnu is said to have had ten 'incarnations', or *avatars*, sometimes appearing in animal form, sometimes in human form. The two most popular incarnations – and, therefore, objects of devotion – are Rama (of *Romance of Rama* fame) and Krishna (of *Bhagavad-gita* fame).

Vishnu is thought to embody the *preserving* qualities of *Brahman*. He and his incarnations are thus worshipped as the deities who are active in society for good. Through devotion to

Vishnu the faithful hope eventually to escape birth-and-rebirth and experience 'release'.

Devotion to Siva (Saivism)

Saivism is the term used to describe the many groups in India that devote themselves to the god Siva and his various incarnations. Again, in the great epics of the 'remembered writings' (*smriti*) worshippers find ample reasons to praise and revere this god.

Siva is quite different from Vishnu, even though both shine forth as aspects of *Brahman*. Whereas Vishnu is the friend and preserver of humanity, Siva is the multifaceted master over nature and human beings. He is not responsible to anyone or anything and is capable of unpredictable acts of domination. In the stories about him he can be both a mystical ascetic and an erotic lover. He can strike down and he can spare. It is no wonder, despite his unpredictable character, that Siva has enjoyed a huge following for over two millennia. As a personal digression, before I became convinced about the claims of Christ, I learnt martial arts from a group of Hindus here in Sydney. During those years, I myself offered the occasional prayer and act of worship to Siva.

As another Trivial Pursuit™ aside, teachers from a branch of *Saivism* during the AD 1200s developed a particular form of yoga (*hatha-yoga*) involving difficult breathing and body exercises. This was thought to bring spiritual oneness with the divine. Various forms and adaptations of this *hatha-yoga* have become immensely popular in the 'yoga' of the West.

Although too brief to give you a very detailed picture of the immense tradition we call Hinduism, these few chapters have tried to give you a taste of the flavoursome, three-part cocktail Indians call the 'Eternal Religion'.

Hinduism in brief

1500–500 BC. Nomadic Aryans settle in India, bringing their *Vedic* religion.
- The four *Vedas*, or books of 'Wisdom' are composed
- Lots of gods (fire, storm, etc.)
- Rituals and sacrifice to keep the gods in favour

1000–300 BC. Indian gurus begin to unpack the meaning of the *Vedas*.
- Most important writings in this period are the *Upanishads*
- *Brahman*: the One force, or 'Flame', of the universe
- *Atman*: the 'soul' as a spark from *Brahman*
- *Samsara*: the trap of earthly existence and re-existence because of *karma*
- *Moksha*: escape back into *Brahman*

300 BC–AD 300. The composition of many so called 'remembered' (*smriti*) writings.
- Most important writing in this period is the *Bhagavad-gita*, or *Song of the Lord*

Four castes of society
  1. Priests
  2. Warrior-kings
  3. Common people
  4. Servants

Three paths to salvation
  1. Do the *duty* of your caste
  2. Attain *knowledge* of your oneness with *Brahman*
  3. Devote yourself to a 'favourite god'

Two major 'schools' of Hinduism
  1. *Vaishnavism* (devotion to Vishnu)
  2. *Saivism* (devotion to Siva)

Facts and figures on Hinduism today
- Hinduism is the third largest religion in the world with over 830 million believers.[1]
- Hindus make up about 13% of the world's population.[2]
- Hinduism is found in 114 countries in the world.[3]
- *Sanskrit*, the language of the Hindu Scriptures, is the mother of all European languages, including English.
- There are an estimated 300 million different gods worshipped in India today.

[1, 2, 3] *Britannica Book of the Year 2004*, Encyclopaedia Britannica Inc. (p 280)

Famous Hindus include:
Mahatma Gandhi
Considered the father of the Indian nation. Famous for his policy of non-violent resistance – crucial in the fight for Indian Independence. Assassinated in 1948.

George Harrison
Beatles guitarist and songwriter. Harrison's search for God began in his mid-20s. It led him to delve deeply into the mystical world of Eastern religions, especially Hinduism, Indian philosophy, culture and music.

Sachin Tendulkar
Indian cricketer regarded as one of the greatest batsmen in the world. Up to July 2004 he had scored 9,470 runs at an average of 57.39 with 37 centuries and a highest score of 241.

Good books and sites on Hinduism
http://www.hindunet.org

http://www.hindu.org

http://www.hinduismtoday.com

Zaehner, R. C., *Hinduism*. Oxford: Oxford University Press, 1966.

Biardeau, M., *Hinduism: the Anthropology of a Civilization* Oxford: Oxford University Press, 1994.

Smart, N. and Hecht, R. (editors), 'Hinduism', in *Sacred Texts of the World: a universal anthology*. New York: Crossroad, 2002, 179–230.

Smart, N., *The World's Religions* (2nd edltion). Cambridge: Cambridge University Press, 2003, 43–102.

Brockington, J. L., *The Sacred Thread: Hinduism in its Continuity and Diversity*. Edinburgh: Edinburgh University Press, 1981.

Hardy, F., 'The Classical Religions of India', in *The World's Religions* (ed. S. Sutherland, et al.). London: Routledge, 1988, 569–645.

Beckerlege, G. (ed.), *World Religions Reader* (2nd edition). London: Routledge, 2001 (Part Four: Hinduism, 201–320).

Feuerstein, G. A., *Introduction to the Bhagavad-Gita: its Philosophy and Cultural Setting*. London: Rider and Company, 1974.

Gotshalk, R., *Bhagavad Gita: Translation and Commentary*. Delhi: Motilal Banarsidass, 1985.

Buddhism
The Way of
Enlightenment

In a nutshell

Buddhism is a practical philosophy first taught by Prince Siddhartha Gautama, otherwise known as the Buddha, or 'enlightened one'. At its heart, Buddhism teaches that the suffering of the world, which is all-pervasive, is the direct result of human desire: desire for wealth, desire for comfort, desire for self-recognition, and so on. By removing such desires – through practising the Buddha's teachings – men and women are able to escape the pain of the world and so experience the tranquillity of enlightenment.

7 Origins of Buddhism

World's most fashionable religion

Buddhism has to take the prize for Today's Most Fashionable Religion. The number of times I hear people say, 'Oh, I like the Buddhist philosophy', is quite amazing.

And, let's face it, there is a lot to like! Think of the Buddhist Richard Gere, that handsome, socially concerned Hollywood star. Then there's the head of Tibetan Buddhism, the Dalai Lama. He's one very likeable guy. He's always happy, always serene, and always filling venues for lectures on his faith. Then, of course, there's the Buddha himself, recognizable to most Westerners as that smiling, contented fellow in the great statues of Asia.

Buddhism is also a religion of peace. Everyone knows Buddhists wouldn't hurt a fly (literally) let alone their fellow human beings. Given the bloody trail of religious history throughout Europe and the Middle East, it's no wonder Buddhism wins the vote for 'Nicest Guy' on the religious block.

Another attraction of Buddhism is its perceived simplicity. I once overheard a group of (quite obviously) non-religious 'twenty-somethings' discussing things spiritual. They were guests at a rather loud dinner party on the balcony next door; and short of leaving the balcony I was on it was difficult *not* to eavesdrop. In the course of the conversation, one of the guests offered a personal evaluation of 'Western religion' compared with 'Eastern religion', and with Buddhism in particular.

'Western religion,' he said with confidence, 'is too full of commandments for me.'

'I prefer the Buddhist system,' he added, 'it doesn't have any of those onerous rules.'

As he sipped his Chardonnay, unaware of the Buddha's views on drinking, the others 'mmm-ed' in agreement. Buddhism, it was decided, is the no-stress, no-strings-attached religion.

The attraction of Buddhism is clear, and it is true that the removal of what we call 'stress' is one of the clear outcomes of the Buddhist path. But it would be a mistake to assume that the teaching of the Buddha himself was 'uncomplicated' and 'undemanding'. In fact, I'm confident that after a little more research readers will agree that Buddhism is probably the most intellectually sophisticated of the great Faiths and also the one requiring the highest level of discipline from its adherents.

The prince who felt pain

The founder of Buddhism was raised in the *sanatana dharma*, or what we call Hinduism. His name was Siddhartha Gautama (sometimes spelt Sidhattha Gottama) and he was an Indian prince of the 'warrior-king' caste of Indian society. There is no doubt the Prince existed, but historical records about his life are not plentiful. Some of the sacred writings place his life in the 500s BC (preferred by most Buddhists); others place him in the 400s BC (preferred by most historians). Take your pick.

The young prince's parents ruled the Indian kingdom of the Sakyas in north-east India (where Nepal is today). It wasn't unusual in those days for a prince – or anyone for that matter – to be married quite young, and Gautama was no exception. At sixteen years of age he married the beautiful Yasodhara.

Palace life for the prince would have been pleasant and safe, well protected from the poverty and sickness experienced by many on the other side of the walls. He had lily ponds to play in, female musicians to entertain him, and three palaces to enjoy at different times of the year.

All of this was to change, however, when around twenty-nine years of age Gautama ventured beyond the palace to inspect his kingdom. According to one tradition, Siddhartha Gautama was overcome with grief at what he saw: a frail old man, a desperately ill man and, finally, a corpse. The next day, says the same tradition, Siddhartha saw a fourth man quite different from the others. This was a sight that would change his life forever. The fourth man was a Hindu 'ascetic' – a guru who had chosen the 'Path of Knowledge' discussed in the previous chapter. So impressed was Gautama by the peaceful look on the teacher's face that the prince decided immediately to give up his life of luxury and set out to discover for himself the secret of serenity in a world of pain.

And, so, before his thirtieth birthday, Siddhartha Gautama left his privileged life, his beautiful wife and his newborn baby, to search for an answer to the troubling dilemma of suffering.

The first path the ex-prince pursued was, naturally enough, the way of asceticism, denying all earthly comforts and striving for meditative states of mystic consciousness. For six long years, say the records, Gautama wandered the region of the Ganges River in north-east India studying the ancient Hindu traditions and submitting himself to the demands of the famous gurus he met along the way. But nothing satisfied. Suffering and evil were still as potent and troubling to Siddhartha as before.

The moment of enlightenment

Having experienced the path of 'luxury' and the path of 'denial', Siddhartha was convinced that neither provided the answer he was looking for. The key to the removal of suffering, he thought, must lie somewhere else. With this thought in mind he committed himself to pondering the dilemma night and day until he found the solution.

One night in May, while sitting under a tree, the answer came to Siddhartha in a moment of pure insight. An important scripture written by Asvaghosa, a second-century (AD) convert to Buddhism, describes the moment well:

Then, as the third watch of that night drew on, the supreme master of trance turned his meditation to the real and essential nature of this world: 'Alas, living beings wear themselves out in vain! Over and over again they are born, they age, die, pass on to a new life, and are reborn! What is more, greed and dark delusion obscure their sight, and they are blind from birth. Greatly apprehensive, they yet do not know how to get out of this great mass of ill.' He then surveyed the twelve lines of conditioned co-production [a complex Buddhist doctrine mentioned in the next chapter], and saw that, beginning with ignorance, they lead to old age and death, and, beginning with the cessation of ignorance, they lead to the cessation of birth, old age, death and all kinds of ill. When the great seer had comprehended that where there is no ignorance whatever, there also the karma-formations are stopped – then he had achieved a correct knowledge of all there is to be known, and he stood out in the world as a Buddha (Buddhacarita, *Discourse on the Acts of Buddha*).

This was the moment of 'enlightenment' for Prince Siddhartha. From that time on he would be known to his disciples as the 'Buddha' ('Enlightened One'). I will adopt this conventional title of respect throughout these chapters.

Siddhartha Gautama had been raised as royalty with the duty of ruling over the people of north-east India, but for the next forty-five years (he is reported to have lived until eighty) he would devote himself exclusively to teaching his insights to all who would listen.

After Gautama's death, his teachings were preserved in spoken-form through a process of memorization and proclamation (conducted mainly in monasteries). The material was eventually written down sometime in the first century BC. Despite this 300–400 year time gap between the Buddha's life and the first Buddhist writings, the intellectual sophistication and uniqueness of the Buddha still shines through these sacred pages.

8 Buddha's critique of Hinduism

Some of Siddhartha Gautama's insights under that tree (known as the *Bodhi-tree*, or 'tree of wisdom') were what you might call *innovations* in religious thinking: new religious ideas. Some of them, however, involved *rejections* of the religion he grew up with. Before we look at what Siddhartha proposed, let's look at what he threw out.

The 'Middle Path'

Siddhartha Gautama had experienced both pleasure and deprivation. In his view, neither of these extremes led to true insight. Both were paths of ignorance, he insisted. In his Indian context, this amounted to a rejection of the two extremes of Hindu religion (as he saw it). What Siddhartha proposed in their place was called the 'Middle Path' (*Majjhima Patipada*). It got this name not because it was a happy balance between two extremes – a little bit of pleasure and a little bit of pain – but because it dismissed both paths altogether. The Buddha's first sermon (from *Vinaya, Mahavagga*) declares:

Monks, these two extremes should not be followed... (1) Devotion to the pleasures of sense... and (2) devotion to self-mortification which is painful, unworthy and unprofitable. By avoiding these two extremes the Tathagata (a title for Buddha) has gained knowledge of that middle path which gives vision, which gives knowledge, which causes calm, special knowledge, enlightenment, Nibbana [Nirvana].

The caste system

Another aspect of Hinduism that Siddhartha rejected was the belief in the four castes. Although born into the privileged Indian caste of the 'warrior-king', Prince Gautama refused to make any distinction between members of the human race. He mixed with all, taught all, and was adamant that everyone – including lowly 'servants', or *sudras* – could reach the highest goal of his teaching.

The role of the Brahmans

Related to this 'egalitarian' view of society was Siddhartha's insistence that the *Brahmans* (Hindu priests), with their rituals and speculative philosophy, were as ignorant about the truth as anyone else. Some of the most scathing criticisms in Siddhartha's teachings are reserved for this particular class of Indian society:

> *Then, it is like a line of blind men, each holding on to the preceding one; the first one does not see, the middle one also does not see, the last one also does not see. Thus, it seems to me that the state of the Brahmans is like that of a line of blind men* (Canki Sutta, Majjhima Nikaya 95).

God, the soul and the self

Earlier in the book we discussed the Hindu belief that each living being, including humans, possesses an *atman*, the soul, or real You, behind your simple everyday consciousness. This *atman* is a 'spark', says Hinduism, from the eternal 'Flame' which is *Brahman*, that ultimate Reality behind the universe.

Siddhartha Gautama rejected these fundamental Hindu ideas. He regarded teachings about 'God' (or ultimate Reality) and the 'soul' as pure guess-work and completely irrelevant to the path of wisdom. He didn't come out and say, 'Friends, there is no God in the universe.' Thus, it might not be accurate to describe him as an 'atheist' (one who believes that God does not exist). He simply dismissed such questions outright. In his view, they were ignorant and foolish matters. He was, if you like, a *practical* atheist if not a theoretical one.

But things get more complex, I'm afraid. Not only did Siddhartha think there was no eternal 'soul' worth worrying about – whether a human soul or a divine one – he believed there was no actual *you* to think about either. You might want to pause here and let this thought occupy your mind for a moment: a key to Buddhism is the belief that YOU (and John Dickson) do not ultimately exist.

The Buddhist argument here is difficult to follow and a little counter-intuitive, but it is brilliant. Gautama said that the thing you call 'you' is really just a combination of ever-changing physical and mental activities going on in the same space (your body and brain). These activities are the result, said Siddhartha, of physical and mental activities that occurred a moment earlier. These, in turn, are the result of ones that occurred a moment before that, and so on. There is no 'you' arising from this chain of cause-and-effect. There is just the chain itself – just physical and mental activities causing further physical and mental activities. The thing you think of as 'you' is just a fantasy, taught Gautama, born of ignorance. It is an illusion.

For Buddhism, this is not just a brain-teaser designed to mystify students of religion; it is in fact a key to the Buddhist life. The goal of Buddhism is to help people realize that they do not ultimately exist. Once we realize this fact, and live accordingly, we will have become 'enlightened'. But more about that later.

The Five Aggregates of Attachment

For now I need to unpack a related and complex Buddhist teaching known officially as the 'Five Aggregates of Attachment', that is, the five ways in which people attach themselves both to the world at large and to the idea of the *self*. Frankly, when writing this chapter I debated whether I should include this section. I wanted to save readers from further brain strain. But Siddhartha Gautama himself would have insisted I keep it in. So, to honour the great man's intentions, let me offer a spectator's version of the 'Five Aggregates'.

The idea behind the 'Five Aggregates of Attachment' is that there are *five basic factors in the human person*, all of which are constantly changing, none of which can be called a continuing 'you', and all of which go to make up the illusion of the human *self*. Got it? Right, here are the five factors:

1. Matter (*rupa*). The first and most obvious factor in the thing you think of as your *self* is the material factor – physical matter, sights, odours, sounds, etc. Included here are the four traditional Buddhist elements of earth, air, fire and water. This physical existence, along with some brain functions, make up part of the illusion you call you.

2. Sensation (*vedana*). When material elements in the world bump into other material elements in the human body 'sensations' arise. For instance, an odour up my nose might result in the sensation of 'smell'. Again, a sound in my ear might result in the sensation of 'sound'. Sensations of happiness and sadness are also included in this category, since they too are often just the effects of material causes.

3. Perception (*samjna*). 'Perception', said Siddhartha, is the *recognition* of physical or mental functions. For example, I might recognize a certain smell to be the smell of my body odour. Again, I might recognize a certain sound as the sound of music. I have no control over my perceptions. They are just 'reflex' realizations resulting from 'matter' and 'sensations'.

4. Mental Formations (*samskara*). Whenever I direct my mind towards a particular thought or action I am experiencing a 'mental formation', said Siddhartha. For example, upon perceiving my own body odour I might *decide* to have a bath. Again, upon perceiving the sound of music I might decide to turn up the volume. These decisions, or acts of the will, are 'mental formations'. Mental formations also include things like *concentration*, forcing your mind to think about one thing for a time (you might be finding that particular 'mental formation' quite difficult right now). Mental formations also include decisions of the will such as *desire, hate, jealousy*, and so on. It's important to appreciate, however, that in Gautama's

view there is no 'you' directing these mental formations; there are just the formations themselves.

5. Consciousness (*vijnana*). At first, this aggregate is difficult to differentiate from 'perception' (the third aggregate), but there is a difference. 'Perception' recognizes things as *particular things* (odour, sound, etc.). 'Consciousness' is simply an 'awareness' of the presence and characteristics of a thing (whether physical or mental). To continue the examples we've been using: 'consciousness' is the *awareness* of a smell that is unpleasant, whereas 'perception' identifies the smell as, say, my body odour; again, 'consciousness' is the *awareness* of a sound with certain tones and volumes, whereas 'perception' identifies that sound as the sound of music.

The details of the 'Five Aggregates' might seem complex, but the important thing to realize about this teaching is its *purpose*. Siddhartha is taking the thing we usually think of as the *self* and breaking it down into its component parts. By doing this, he demonstrates that there is no 'self' after all; there is just a chain of cause-and-effect operating within these five aspects of the human being. There is no enduring you, just the illusion caused by these five ever-changing, arising and disappearing 'factors' of human experience. Put another way, the sum of the parts does not make up a greater whole called the *self*; all that exists are the parts.

There is another Buddhist concept that seeks to map out the process by which the illusion of the 'self' arises in each person. It is called 'Conditioned Arising (or Co-production)' and it has twelve stages, beginning with *ignorance*. Each of these stages then breaks down into various component parts. If you want to explore this theme further, most of the books mentioned at the end of the chapter provide careful accounts.

For now, it is probably helpful to put the point crudely, but no less accurately. According to the teaching of the 'Five Aggregates of Attachment', there is no Thinker, there are just thoughts; there is no Smeller, there are just acts of smelling; there is no Listener, there are just acts of listening. In short, there is no 'you' at all.

Please note: throughout his teaching Buddha still used words like 'I', 'you', 'he', 'oneself', and so on. This is not a contradiction of his No-Self doctrine. Pronouns such as these were still required, believed the Buddha, in order to refer to those entities which (the Buddhist knows) in reality possess no enduring Self. They are short-hand, if you like, for talking about that collection of matter, sensations, perceptions, mental formations and consciousness that people (wrongly) think of as themselves.

Why is it so important in Buddhism to remove the notion of the 'self'? Because in Buddha's view the idea of the *self* is the root of all suffering. It is your (and my) desire for *self*-satisfaction, *self*-existence and *self*-advancement that creates the experience of pain. Remove the *self*, that is, realize there never was such a thing, and suffering will evaporate. This is the heart of Buddhism and we're going to say a lot more about it in a later chapter.

Rebirth versus reincarnation

If there is no 'soul' or 'you', then clearly there can be no reincarnation, at least, not in the full Hindu sense of a continuing *self* re-existing after death in another body. Although Buddhism and Hinduism are often lumped together in their views of the afterlife, they are in fact quite different.

Siddhartha Gautama taught an idea known simply as 'rebirth'. Rebirth does not involve getting a new body for an old soul; it is just the continuation of the five factors of existence (the Five Aggregates) in a long chain of cause-and-effect. Let me explain. Since every human 'sensation', 'perception' and 'mental formation' is determined by prior 'sensations', 'perceptions' and 'mental formations', Gautama argued that rebirth must also work like this. The final 'sensation', 'perception' and 'mental formation' of *this* life determines the first 'sensation', 'perception' and 'mental formation' of the *next* life. For Siddhartha, existence is just one long chain of cause-and-effect, and death does not end that chain.

So far, we have been exploring what the Buddha rejected from his Hindu heritage – the caste system, God, the idea of the *self*, the doctrine of reincarnation, and so on. More significant by far, however, is what he discovered in his 'enlightenment' and then proclaimed for the next forty-five years.

9 The Four Noble Truths

Almost everything Siddhartha Gautama taught in his long career was an exposition of four *beliefs* and eight *habits*. This makes memorizing the Buddhist system (which is not the same as understanding it, of course!) relatively easy. The four beliefs are known as the 'Four Noble Truths'. The eight habits are known as the 'Eightfold Path'. Let's now unpack these (4 + 8 =) 12 essentials of Buddhism.

We've already seen that Siddhartha Gautama was motivated from the start by a search for peace in the midst of a world of suffering. The 'Four Noble Truths' are all about experiencing this tranquility.

First Noble Truth: suffering exists

The 'First Noble Truth' is easy to understand. It involves simply acknowledging the existence and nature of suffering.

The word used by Siddhartha to summarize the 'First Noble Truth' is *dukkha*. *Dukkha*, however, has a much broader meaning than the English word 'suffering'. One major book on Buddhism (published by Oxford University Press) even avoids translating *dukkha*. Throughout the book this scholar writes: '*Dukkha* this' and '*Dukkha* that'. It gets pretty confusing. In my opinion, as long as we keep in mind that 'suffering' in Buddhist thought is a bigger concept than we're used to, the English word will do just fine. Here's the Buddha's own description of *dukkha* and the First Noble Truth:

> *Now this, monks, is the noble truth about suffering (dukkha):*
> *Birth is suffering, decay is suffering, sickness is suffering, death is*

suffering: likewise sorrow and grief, woe, lamentation and despair.
To be conjoined with things which we dislike; to be separated from
things which we like – that also is suffering. Not to get what one
wants – that also is suffering. In a word, this body, this fivefold
mass which is based on grasping-that is suffering (The First
Sermon: Vinaya, Mahavagga*).*

For Gautama, *dukkha* refers to just about everything in life, not
only to pain and hardship but also to the fleeting nature of
existence. Everything is momentary, here-today-gone-
tomorrow. In this sense, the Buddha can even describe positive
experiences as suffering because they tend to evaporate shortly
after they appear. Anyone who has experienced an emotional
'high' only to come down to a great 'low' will know what the
Buddha meant.

According to Gautama, the 'Five Aggregates of Attachment'
are also suffering. What he means by this is not difficult to see.
If everything you think of as 'you' is simply a series of 'effects'
produced by prior 'causes' (which themselves are the product
of earlier causes) then unenlightened existence itself, by its
very nature, is tragic. It is *dukkha*.

The First Noble Truth, then, is the recognition that suffering
exists in all these forms.

Second Noble Truth: the origin of suffering

The 'Second Noble Truth' tries to explain the *origin* of suffering.
Siddhartha's logic is powerful. Suffering, says the Buddha,
arises in your life because of 'desire' or 'craving'. At its most
basic level, the logic goes like this. If you crave riches, poverty
will feel painful to you. If you desire comfort, discomfort will
trouble you. Think about it for a moment; it's hard to argue
with! Here are the Buddha's words:

Now this, monks, is the noble truth about the arising of suffering:
It is that craving that leads back to birth, along with the lure and
the lust that lingers longingly now here, now there: namely, the
craving for sensual pleasure, the craving to be born again, the

craving for existence to end. Such, monks, is the noble truth about the arising of suffering (The First Sermon: Vinaya, Mahavagga*)*.

For Siddhartha, craving comes in several forms. Firstly, there is desire for 'sense-pleasures'. This includes craving for wealth, comfort, physical gratification, and so on. Secondly, there is the desire for 'existence'. When people are ignorant of the teaching about the 'Five Aggregates' they live under the false impression that they possess a continuing 'self'. They nurse this 'self' and strive to prolong its experience. They long for re-existence. Such craving for existence, thought Gautama, is the cause of much suffering.

The third type of desire is the craving for non-existence. This may seem illogical at first. If craving for existence is wrong why would craving for the opposite be wrong as well? Basically, because *craving* is the problem, not the thing craved for.

Karma and the Second Noble Truth

Before we move on to the Third Noble Truth, it might be helpful to pause and say something about the Buddhist understanding of *karma*, which is similar but not identical to the Hindu idea of *karma*.

Within Buddhism *karma* usually refers to *wilful action*, or actions that grow out of your desires/cravings. There is such a thing as non-wilful action which we'll look at in a moment.

A morally good action will produce a good effect, and a morally bad action will produce a bad effect. In both cases an action produces an *onward* effect. That is in the nature of *karma*; it is just how the universe works, said the Buddha.

It would be a mistake, however, to think that the goal of Buddhism is simply to do good deeds in an effort to produce good effects. According to Buddhism, even good actions producing good effects are part of the sad chain of cause-and-effect. Why? Because even the best things in life are fleeting. Beauty fades, pleasure dissipates, and joy passes. And when this happens regret and sadness emerge, proving that life is just a long line of arising-disappearing-arising-disappearing. For Buddha, then, even relatively 'good *karma*' producing relatively 'good outcomes' is ultimately tragic (*dukkha*).

The greatest tragedy in all this is that the effects of wilful action (of *karma*) don't cease at death. Karma produces rebirth. Rebirth brings yet more of the fleeting and painful aspects of life. You are trapped, and it is all the fault of *karma*, of acting out of craving.

The perfected Buddhist, however, is free from the idea of Self, and so is able to live in the world without any craving whatsoever. Without craving, action accumulates no *karma*. Without *karma*, there is no rebirth. Problem solved. The Buddhist who achieves this perfected level is called an *Arhat*, a 'worthy one'. More about that in a moment.

The Second Noble Truth describes the relationship between craving, *karma* and suffering. This is the 'bad news' of Buddhism. The *good* news is contained in the Third Noble Truth.

Third Noble Truth: the end of suffering

Once you have understood the existence of suffering ('First Noble Truth') and have understood its root cause ('Second Noble Truth'), the removal of suffering follows naturally, if not very easily. Suffering disappears when you get rid of 'desire'.

And this, monks, is the noble truth about the ceasing of suffering: It is the complete cessation of that very craving, giving it up, relinquishing it, liberating oneself from it, and detaching oneself from it (The First Sermon: Vinaya, Mahavagga).

This is the 'Third Noble Truth': the realization that the end of suffering comes through the elimination of human cravings.

Nirvana and the Third Noble Truth

At this point I'd like to introduce the Buddhist idea of *Nirvana*, a word which means 'blowing out' or 'extinction'. *Nirvana* is not a heavenly place, or a peaceful state of mind. It is the extinguishment of all desire – whether the desire for pleasure, for existence, or for non-existence. Put another way, *Nirvana* is the realization that the Self does not really exist, and that human desire is therefore empty. A person who has come to this realization is able to act in this world with complete detachment, that is, without desire. His or her actions are without *karma*. The person who attains the state of *Nirvana* has escaped the world of cause-and-effect and is free from the cycle of birth and rebirth.

Is *Nirvana* a negative idea? Within a Buddhist framework, not at all. How could the realization of reality – of the way things really are – be considered negative? Only an *un*enlightened person would consider the extinction of the false idea of Self and the eradication of craving as negative. *Nirvana* is neither positive nor negative. It is just the truth, said Buddha.

Will the realization of *Nirvana* be a happy experience? Yes, says the Buddhist, but not in the normal Western sense of the word 'happy'. If by 'happy' you mean a 'sensation' or 'feeling' of joy then, no, *Nirvana* is not a happy experience. Remember, emotional sensations are always dependent upon something else; they are part of this arising-disappearing world. The happiness of *Nirvana* is the true joy of having realized the ultimate Truth. It is the bliss of escaping the endless chain of cause-and-effect.

Nirvana is fully realized at death, when the physical body of the enlightened person ceases functioning. However, it can also be experienced before death. There are four stages in the Buddhist life, each with its own increasing realization of *Nirvana*:

1. The 'Stream-entrant', or novice, only catches a glimpse of *Nirvana* in the teaching of the Buddha.

2. The 'Once-Returner', as the name suggests, is destined to be reborn in this physical world just one more time before experiencing full *Nirvana*.

3. The 'Never-Returner' has an even deeper knowledge of *Nirvana* and is assured that he or she will not be 'reborn'.

4. The 'Worthy-One' (*Arhat*) is totally pure and completely free from desire. Such a person has experienced *Nirvana* here and now, and will know it fully at death, when all matter, sensations, perceptions, mental formations and consciousness will disappear forever.

The Third Noble Truth is simply this: if you eradicate your craving for all things (pleasure, existence and non-existence) suffering evaporates.

It is easy to see how this might work in theory. If you live with complete detachment from the world, and even from the idea of Self, almost by definition you will feel unaffected by the changing fortunes of life. Hardship will not trouble you, since you have no desire for comfort. Poverty will not disappoint you, for you do not crave wealth. Personal insults will not hurt, because you are detached from the very idea of your Self. This is the logic behind the tranquility Westerners often observe in Buddhists. Here are the Buddha's own words about 'detachment' and the end of suffering:

> *A learned and noble disciple… becomes dispassionate with regard to the body… with regard to tangible things… He becomes dispassionate with regard to the mind… Being dispassionate, he becomes detached; through detachment he is liberated. When liberated there is knowledge that he is liberated. And he knows: Birth (i.e., rebirth) is exhausted, the holy life has been lived, what has to be done is done, there is no more left to be done on this account (The Fire Sermon,* Adittapariyaya Sutta: Samyutta Nikaya 35).

However, Siddhartha Gautama admitted that the removal of desire and the attainment of such tranquility are not easy goals. People do not just hear the first three Noble Truths and suddenly realize *Nirvana*. People need a path, a method of cultivating the thoughts and actions conducive to this realization. That's what the Fourth Noble Truth is all about.

Fourth Noble Truth: the path to the end of suffering

Although Buddhism is highly intellectual, it is also very practical. Buddhist writers sometimes criticize Western writers on Buddhism (like me) for wrongly emphasizing the philosophical over the practical. The path of the Buddha, insist Buddhists themselves, is a practical way of living in the world just as much as it is a comprehensive way of *thinking* about the world. The Fourth Noble Truth bears this out.

Earlier in the chapter I said that almost everything the Buddha taught can be understood as an exposition of four basic *beliefs* (or 'Noble Truths') and eight basic *habits*. It turns out that the Fourth Noble Truth is the teaching about the eight basic habits.

> Now this, monks, is the noble truth about the practice that leads to the cessation of suffering: It is this noble eightfold way, namely, right understanding, right aim, right speech, right action, right livelihood, right effort, right mindfulness, right concentration
> (*The First Sermon:* Vinaya, Mahavagga).

The eight basic habits are known collectively as the Eightfold Path. They are not, however, just eight random rules for gaining enlightenment. They are expressions of the three essential categories of the Buddhist way of life:

1. *Wisdom.* Two of the habits in the 'Eightfold Path' fall into the category of 'wisdom'. These habits are designed to enhance your appreciation of the 'truths' of Buddhism, truths such as the 'Five Aggregates', 'Karma', the 'Four Noble Truths' and so on.

2. *Ethical conduct.* Three of the eight habits promote the *lifestyle* Buddha said was necessary for removing 'desire' and experiencing *Nirvana*. These habits are all 'ethical' in nature. That is, they have to do with morality.

3. *Mental Discipline.* The final three habits are thinking-exercises, or what are called 'mental disciplines', designed to cultivate the thought life required for attaining *Nirvana*.

With these three categories of the Buddhist life in mind, let's now unpack the Eightfold Path, the path designed to bring us to the full realization of *Nirvana*.

10 The Eightfold Path

The Eightfold Path contains the habits of life that are necessary for seeing things as they really are. By practising this path the Buddhist is able to remove all craving and so bring an end to all 'karma-formations'. Such a person is free from the need to be reborn.

In the category of wisdom are two habits.

First habit: right understanding

A Buddhist is required to cultivate a correct understanding of Siddhartha's teaching. In its most basic form, this aspect of the Eightfold Path involves gaining a thorough knowledge of the Four Noble Truths. Since these concepts are found in the Buddhist Scriptures themselves, study of the sacred Buddhist texts is essential for 'right understanding'. You can't gain 'right understanding', as the Buddha conceived of it, just by reading about Buddhism in a book like this.

Second habit: right aim

A Buddhist must not let thoughts arise and disappear at random. This would be a sign that one was still trapped in the fleeting nature of existence. Instead, the faithful are to aspire to Buddhist ideals. This is 'right aim', and it involves directing your mind towards detachment from the world, compassion toward other creatures, and so on.

The following three parts of the Eightfold Path have to do with ethical conduct.

Third habit: right speech

Buddhists are to 'speak' in a way consistent with the removal of desire and the eradication of the idea of 'self'. They are to refrain from lying, slandering and being rude. To do otherwise would be to act with craving – with a commitment to 'self'.

Fourth habit: right action

The followers of Gautama are also to act in a way consistent with the negation of 'desire'. Buddhists are therefore to reject dishonest dealings and steer clear of all illegitimate sexual contact. Buddhists must not kill or injure other living creatures, and they are to avoid all consumption of alcohol. Buddhists are also to seek to help others lead honourable lives. Again, to do otherwise would be inconsistent with the ideal of detachment so important to the Buddhist outlook.

Fifth habit: right livelihood

The fifth aspect of the path has to do with the kinds of employment Buddhists are allowed to pursue. A Buddhist must find a profession that does no harm to other creatures. This rules out jobs involving the trade of weapons, engagement in warfare, the promotion of alcohol and the killing of animals. Such jobs arise from, and foster, human craving and the false notion of 'self'.

Concrete expression of right speech, right action and right livelihood is found in the so-called Five Precepts – the Buddhist equivalent of the biblical Ten Commandments. These precepts provide the bare minimum required of the Buddhist: (1) to abstain from taking life; (2) to refrain from stealing; (3) to avoid sexual immorality; (4) to refrain from lying; (5) to abstain from all intoxicants (alcohol, drugs).

In the category of 'mental discipline' are the three remaining habits of the Eightfold Path.

Sixth habit: right effort

Buddhists are meant to engage daily in an energetic decision to put an end to false thoughts and unwholesome states of mind (including the thought of 'self'), and they are to *make every effort* to promote healthy states of mind. You cannot just drift along in the Buddhist life; you must be diligent. Without right effort no progress will be made in the journey toward enlightenment.

Seventh habit: right mindfulness

For Westerners, this aspect of the Buddhist path may seem unusual and introspective. Buddhists are to strive to be *aware* of everything that goes on around them and within them – every sound, every bodily sensation, every fleeting thought or emotion, and so on. More than that, the Buddhist must try to be aware of how such sensations and emotions arise and disappear.

By noticing this arising-and-disappearing the Buddhist enhances his or her appreciation of Siddhartha's teaching about the Five Aggregates of Attachment. The Buddhist begins to realize that the thing we call the 'self' is really just a passing illusion of interacting bodies, sensations, mental formations, and so on.

Eighth habit: right concentration

Meditation is an essential aspect of Buddhist life. By 'meditation', however, Buddhists don't just mean the 'transcendental' kind we find in the Hindu tradition (Siddhartha had tried his form of meditation and found it to be inadequate for enlightenment). The meditation taught by Gautama basically involves deep concentration.

There are two types of meditation in Buddhist tradition. First, there is In-and-Out Breathing mediation. This involves sitting upright with legs crossed and attempting to become fully aware of your own breathing. This is designed to enhance your powers of concentration.

On first hearing, the second type of meditation doesn't sound much like meditation at all. It involves a concentrated awareness of all daily conduct. Think of it as an intense version of 'right mindfulness'. When running, for example, you are to concentrate on the movement of your legs, the pattern of your breathing and any other related sensation. You must not think in terms of you running. Rather, you are to focus only on the act of running itself, with all its connected sensations. The same type of meditation, or concentration, can be practised while washing up, doing home-work, or even while going to the toilet (this last example was suggested by Siddhartha himself).

In all of this, the critical aspect of 'right concentration' is thinking about all sensations and thoughts in terms of their fleeting character – the way they arise and disappear. Once you have lost the sense of 'self' in this analysis (leaving only an awareness of the actions themselves) you are well on your way to *Nirvana*.

The *Zen* Buddhist tradition, popular in Japan and in the West, is an extension of this meditative dimension of the Buddha's teaching. 'Zen' means *meditation*, and this tradition emphasizes the power of certain meditative techniques to bring full enlightenment.

In explaining 'right concentration' Buddha describes the four meditative states a Buddhist will pass through in his or her journey to enlightenment:

Herein a monk, aloof from sense desires, aloof from unwholesome thoughts, (1) attains to and abides in the first meditative state (jhana) which is detachment-born and accompanied by applied thought, sustained thought, joy, and bliss. (2) By allaying applied and sustained thought he attains to, and abides in the second meditative state which is inner tranquillity, which is unification (of the mind), devoid of applied and sustained thought, and which has joy and bliss.

(3) By detachment from joy he dwells in equanimity, mindful, and with clear comprehension and enjoys bliss in body, and

attains to and abides in the third meditative state which the noble ones call: 'Dwelling in equanimity, mindfulness, and bliss.' (4) By giving up of bliss and suffering, by the disappearance already of joy and sorrow, he attains to, and abides in the fourth meditative state, which is neither suffering nor bliss, and which is the purity of equanimity-mindfulness. This is called right concentration (Saccavibhanga Sutta, Majjhima Nikaya *141*).

You will notice that the Eightfold Path has little to do with prayer, worship of a god and religious ceremonies. For this reason, some Buddhists avoid calling their way of life a 'religion' at all. The Eightfold Path is all about attaining a realization of 'the way things are' (as Buddhism presents it). Through these mental and moral practices the Buddhist aims to remove craving and so escape the world of suffering and the need for rebirth.

11 Types of Buddhism

The 'Four Noble Truths' and the 'Eightfold Path' are agreed upon by all Buddhists – after all, these were the core of Siddhartha Gautama's message. Nevertheless, in the period after Gautama's death Buddhist groups, many living in monasteries, began to disagree over various points of belief and practice. Some groups, for instance, attempted to reinstate the idea of a 'self'; others argued over the exact nature of *karma*; still others differed simply over which texts should be regarded as sacred.

Two main schools of Buddhism eventually emerged out of the ancient Buddhist debate. These are the dominant Buddhisms of today and each has its own way of interpreting and applying the great man's teaching.

Theravada Buddhism

The 'Theravada' ('School of the Elders') tradition is usually described as 'classical' Buddhism, the form of Buddhism that is more ancient and original. This description is not without warrant. So far as historians can tell, the Theravadin tradition emphasizes what appear to be the earliest, most authentic teachings of Siddhartha Gautama and his first disciples. Having said this, we need to keep in mind that non-Theravadin Buddhists would dispute this description.

Theravada Buddhism is found mainly in Sri Lanka, Burma, Laos, Cambodia and Thailand. At least four things distinguish this 'school' from other types of Buddhism.

1. *Small collection of Scriptures (or 'canon')*. Firstly, the group of texts Theravadins regard as true scripture (their 'canon') is relatively small compared with other forms of Buddhism. The

Theravadin canon is preserved in the Pali language and is known as the 'The Three Baskets' (*Tipitaka*). Three types of texts are included here (hence, the name): rules about living in a Buddhist monastery, sayings and sermons attributed to Siddhartha himself, and philosophical reflections on Buddhist teachings.

Do other Buddhists recognize the Theravada Scriptures? Yes and no. *Non*-Theravadins regard Theravadin texts as 'sacred' but *incomplete*. They also insist that the texts should be read in Sanskrit translation, not the Pali translation of the Theravadins.

2. *Everything is within you.* Secondly, Theravada Buddhism is confident that *Nirvana* is experienced solely through individual human effort. There is no outside help from a god or mystical power in this form of Buddhism; 'salvation' comes from within your own moral and mental powers. The *Dhammapada*, a favourite Theravadin text, sums it up well:

> *By oneself is wrong done, by oneself is one defiled. By oneself wrong is not done. By oneself, surely, one is cleansed. One cannot purify another; Purity and impurity are in oneself alone* (Dhammapada *165*).

3. *No gods or worship.* Related to this second point, Theravada Buddhists tend to adopt the atheistic viewpoint of Siddhartha Gautama himself. Whereas some Buddhist traditions revere all manner of spiritual beings – some even worship the Buddha himself-Theravadins regard such practices as misguided. They revere Siddhartha as a perfect man but not in any way as a divine being.

4. *Monks and laymen.* Theravada Buddhism tends to emphasize a distinction between the ordained Buddhist monk and the ordinary Buddhist man or woman (the 'layperson'). Many in this tradition believe that only monks can (in the course of this life) fully attain the detachment from craving which is necessary to realize *Nirvana*.

Mahayana Buddhism

'Mahayana' ('Great Vehicle') Buddhism is the name given to a variety of Buddhist groups with certain beliefs and practices in common. This form of Buddhism is dominant in Tibet, China, Japan and Korea, and appears to have developed sometime between 100 BC and AD 100, that is, 400–500 years after Siddhartha Gautama's death. Mahayana Buddhism is characterized by the following elements.

1. *Large collection of Scriptures (canon)*. Firstly, Mahayana Buddhism has a vast collection of sacred texts. Key here are certain additions to the original discourses of the Buddha. Whereas Theravadin Buddhism was concerned to preserve only statements of the *historical* Gautama (and those of his immediate circle of disciples), the Mahayana tradition believes that the teaching of the Buddha was ongoing. During meditation or dreams certain monks could receive revelations from the Buddha revealing truths not previously comprehended. These were believed to be just as valid as the words of the earthly Gautama himself.

When asked why Siddhartha did not teach the Mahayana doctrines during his life, Mahayana Buddhists explain that people in his day were not capable of appreciating the deeper truths of Buddhism. The deepest teachings had to be delayed until the world was ready. One classic Mahayana text puts it this way:

> The Buddha (during his life), knowing that our minds delighted in inferior things, by his tactfulness taught according to our capacity... If we had had a mind to take pleasure in the Great, the Buddha would have preached the Great Vehicle (Mahayana) Law to us (Lotus Sutra, Saddharmapundarika Sutra 4).

We are right to detect here a not-so-subtle critique of the Theravada Buddhist tradition.

2. *A 'celestial' Buddha*. As I said earlier, Theravada Buddhism honours Gautama as the ideal man. Mahayana Buddhism goes beyond this and teaches that the man Siddhartha Gautama was an incarnation of a celestial, heavenly Buddha

who exists throughout time. Mahayana Buddhists serve the Buddha as a divine figure able to assist the faithful in their pursuit of enlightenment. Images of the Buddha, such as those found throughout Asia, are regarded as true objects of worship. Buddhists bring offerings to them and bow down before them. Doing so achieves great spiritual merit, according to the Mahayana tradition.

The Lotus Sutra, one of the most popular Mahayana Scriptures, describes in rapturous detail the heavenly glory of the Buddha. The setting is a vast crowd of human (and divine) beings gathering around the Buddha to hear his words:

At one time the Buddha was in Rajagriha, staying on Mount Gridhrakuta (in North East India). Accompanying him were a multitude of leading monks numbering twelve thousand persons... There were also the sons of gods Rare Moon, Pervading Fragrance, Jeweled Glow, and the Four Great Heavenly Kings, along with their followers, ten thousand sons of gods... At that time the World-Honored One (the Buddha), surrounded by the four kinds of believers, received offerings and tokens of respect and was honored and praised. And for the sake of the bodhisattvas he preached the Great Vehicle (Mahayana teaching)... When the Buddha had finished preaching this Sutra (sermon), he sat with his legs crossed in lotus position... At that time heaven rained down mandarava flowers, great mandarava flowers, manjushaka flowers, and great manjushaka flowers, scattering them over the Buddha and over the great assembly, and everywhere the Buddha world quaked and trembled in six different ways... All those in the great assembly, having gained what they had never had before, were filled with joy and, pressing their palms together, gazed at the Buddha with a single mind. At that time the Buddha emitted a ray of light from the tuft of white hair between his eyebrows, one of his characteristic features, lighting up eighteen thousand worlds in the eastern direction. There was no place that the light did not penetrate (Lotus Sutra, Saddharmapundarika Sutra 1).

From the point of view of the history of religion, it is fascinating that the world's only atheistic Faith (early Theravada

Buddhism) was transformed over time into the full-blown theistic spirituality that is Mahayana Buddhism. Such is the longing of the human heart, it seems, to revere someone greater than ourselves.

Mahayana Buddhism also accepts the existence of many divine beings in addition to Buddha himself – several of them make an appearance in the passage just quoted. Traditions of magic, astrology and divination have also found a place in the Mahayana spirituality.

3. *Delaying Nirvana: the Bodhisattva-path.* It was explained earlier that the highest goal of Buddhism is *Nirvana*, the extinction of all desire and escape from rebirth. This is not entirely true for Mahayanists. Even better than attaining *Nirvana* immediately is the life of the *Bodhisattva* (buddha-to-be).

A *Bodhisattva* is a person who, although qualified to escape rebirth, decides to put off the attainment of *Nirvana* in order to be reborn in this world for the sake of others. The logic is simple. The world is largely ignorant of the Buddha's message and so is trapped in the sphere of suffering (*dukkha*). What the world needs, therefore, are people who are willing to delay their own glory, remain in the world, and lead others to salvation. Mahayanists regard this course as the ultimate expression of compassion.

The Buddhist who chooses the *Bodhisattva*-path begins his journey with a vow. The vow includes the three pledges every Buddhist must make: to Buddha, to the *Dharma* (the Buddha's teaching), and to the *Sangha* (Buddhist community). These are called the Three Jewels, and once you have sincerely declared your devotion to these you are a 'Buddhist'. The *Bodhisattva*, however, goes beyond this threefold vow, promising in addition to strive for *Nirvana* via the longer, compassionate route of the *Bodhisattva*-path. The ideals of this path are described well in a text called The Great Story:

They are Bodhisattvas who live on from life to life (through rebirths) in the possession of manifold good qualities. They are Bodhisattvas who have won the master over karma, and made their deeds renowned through their accumulation of merit… They are devoted to the highest good. They win converts by the means of sympathetic appeal… In all matters they are untiring in their purpose. They are endowed here in this world with the profound attributes of a Buddha… They know how to win the affection of all creatures. When they enter the world they have become endowed with powers that are in accordance with the vows they have made… They are eager to win the sphere of power of a Buddha (The Great Story, Mahavastu*).*

This text refers in passing to another important feature of the *Bodhisattva*-path. Mahayana Buddhism teaches that, after assisting others toward enlightenment and living a life of wisdom and compassion, *Bodhisattvas* will ultimately arrive at 'Buddhahood' themselves. In the words of the text just quoted, they will 'win the sphere of power of a Buddha'. Siddhartha Gautama was a *Bodhisattva* who eventually became an all-knowing Buddha. In the same way, all who follow his path and win sufficient spiritual merit can look forward to the glories of full Buddha existence. Once the *Bodhisattva* has entered Buddhahood his power to assist unenlightened beings will be greatly magnified.

As another Trivial Pursuit™ aside, the spiritual and political leader of Tibet, the Dalai Lama ('Ocean of Wisdom'), is considered to be a shining example of the *Bodhisattva* tradition. The current Dalai Lama, Tenzin Gyatso, is said to be the thirteenth rebirth (and so the fourteenth Dalai Lama) of the original leader of this Tibetan Buddhist order. He has continued to be reborn not because of *karma* but because of his decision to continue sharing the truths of the Buddha with the world.

Actually, the Dalai Lama illustrates another feature of Mahayana Buddhism just mentioned. Tibetan Buddhism has come to regard the Dalai Lama not only as a repeatedly reborn *man* but as a recurring manifestation of one of Mahayana Buddhism's most beloved deities, *Avalokitesvara*. This deity – and therefore also the Dalai Lama – is believed to be a supreme example of compassion. The Nobel Peace Prize, won by Tenzin

Gyatso in 1989, would be considered by Buddhists a testament to this fact.

Theravada (School of the Elders) and Mahayana (Great Vehicle) are the two major forms of Buddhism in the world today. However, I should probably point out that many, many more 'denominations' (or subgroups) exist within these traditions, each with its own perspective and emphasis on the significance of the Buddha's teaching.

Having said that, all Buddhists agree on the essentials of Buddhism outlined earlier. The Four Noble Truths and the Eightfold Path remain the unshakable basis of all Buddhist belief and practice. Through a commitment to these ideas and habits, the Buddhist aims to extinguish craving and so enjoy the tranquility of an existence untouched by the sufferings of the world.

Buddhism in brief

The founder of Buddhism
• Siddhartha Gautama was an Indian prince born around 500 BC
• Siddhartha rejects his native Hindu religion and his life of luxury to discover the solution to the world's suffering
• Enlightenment came one night in May under a 'Bodhi Tree'

The Four Noble Truths: the heart of Gautama's teaching
• Suffering: existence is marred by suffering
• The origin of suffering: suffering arises from 'desire'
• The end of suffering: eradicating 'desire' will release you from suffering and bring the realization of *Nirvana*
• The path to the end of suffering: the way to end desire, and therefore to eradicate suffering, is to practise the eight habits of the Buddhist life

The Eightfold Path: the way to the end of suffering
• Right understanding: knowing the truths of Buddhism
• Right aim: directing the mind to aspire for the ideals of Buddhism
• Right speech: speaking without desire – truthfully, kindly, helpfully
• Right action: acting without desire – non-violently, generously, etc.
• Right livelihood: finding a job fitting to the Buddhist life
• Right effort: energetic daily decision to promote good and true thoughts
• Right mindfulness: diligent awareness of all sensations of body and mind
• Right concentration: practice of Buddhist forms of meditation

Types of Buddhism: the two main 'schools'

Theravada ('School of the Elders'): Often dubbed 'classical Buddhism' this school emphasizes the *historical* man Gautama, and tends to shun mystical speculation.

Mahayana (the 'Great Vehicle'): With a larger canon of scripture, this school encourages devotion to the Buddha as a saviour figure. It also emphasizes the need to postpone *Nirvana* in order to save others from suffering before eventually become a Buddha yourself.

Facts and figures on Buddhism today

• Buddhism is the *fourth* largest religion in the world with over 370 million believers.[1]
• Buddhists make up about 6% of the world's population.[2]
• Buddhism is found in 129 countries in the world.[3]
• Buddhism has had a profound impact on religious and cultural life from China, Korea and Japan in the east, to Afghanistan in the west. It has found a firm footing in South-East Asia and forms an important part of the religious makeup of Europe and North America.

[1, 2, 3] *Britannica Book of the Year 2004*, Encyclopaedia Britannica Inc. (p 280)

Famous Buddhists include:

The Dalai Lama

Tenzin Gyatso was named the fourteenth Dalai Lama in 1937. After the Chinese takeover of Tibet, he was forced into exile. He has spent subsequent years teaching, writing and speaking out for freedom for Tibet, while advocating non-violent resistance. He was granted the Nobel Peace Prize in 1989.

Aung San Suu Kyi

Noted campaigner for democracy and human rights in Myanmar (formerly known as Burma). Aung San Suu Kyi was awarded the Nobel Peace Prize in 1991 for her campaign for peaceful democratic reforms.

Richard Gere
Perhaps the best-known Buddhist in the USA. He has been a long-time supporter of the Dalai Lama and helped organize visits by the Dalai Lama to the USA to give lectures on Buddhism.

Tina Turner
American pop singer who has been a long-time student of Buddhist teaching.

Good books and sites on Buddhism

http://www.buddhanet.net (a site seeking to serve all Buddhist traditions)

http://www.beyondthenet.net (a site mainly from the Theravada Buddhist tradition)

http://www.dharmanet.org

Harvey, P., *An Introduction to Buddhism: Teachings, History and practices*. Cambridge: Cambridge University Press, 1990.

Carter, J. R. and Palihawadana, M. (trans.), *The Dhammapada*. Oxford: Oxford University Press, 2000.

Rahula, W., *What the Buddha Taught* (Revised edition with illustrative texts translated from the original Pali). New York: Grove Press, 1974. (Representing the Theravada tradition)

Gyatso, K. G., *Introduction to Buddhism: an explanation of the Buddhist way of life*. Cumbria: Tharpa Publications, 2002. (Strongly representing the Mahayana tradition)

Smart, N., *The World's Religions* (2nd edition). Cambridge: Cambridge University Press, 2003, 75–165.

Hardy, F., 'The Classical Religions of India', in *The World's Religions* (ed. S. Sutherland, et al.). London: Routledge, 1988, 569–645 ('Buddhism,' 591–603).

Smart, N. and Hecht, R. (editors), 'Buddhism', in *Sacred Texts of the World: a universal anthology*. New York: Crossroad, 2002, 231–275.

Judaism
The Way of
the Torah

In a nutshell

Judaism is the way of life for God's chosen people,
'Israel', otherwise known as the 'Jews'. All important
for the Jew is the Torah, God's instruction, recorded
in the Jewish sacred books known as the Tanak
(what Christians call the Old Testament), Mishnah
and the Talmud. For the Jew, this divine instruction
determines everything – the way you work and rest,
how you study and what you pray for, what you eat
and how you celebrate, and the way you understand
Israel's unique place among non-Jews (or Gentiles).

12 Many Judaisms

Between 1939 and 1945 one-third of all the world's Jews were murdered – that's six million men, women and children brutally killed in just six years. The programme was called *die Endlösung* – The Final Solution. The Chancellor of Germany, Adolf Hitler, sought to rid Europe of all people of Jewish descent (including even German Christians with Jewish ancestry). The Holocaust, as it has become known, probably represents the vilest moment in human history, and marks out the Jews as a unique people – without match both in their depth of suffering and their will to survive.

As we'll soon see, this sense of uniqueness has been part of the Jewish consciousness from the very beginning, ever since God said to Abraham, the founding father of Judaism (1800 BC):

> 'I will make you into a great nation… and all peoples on earth will be blessed through you' (Bereshit [or Genesis] 12:1–3).

Before we explore the unique sufferings and glories of the children of Abraham, I need to clear up some confusion over our modern use of terms like 'Jew' and 'Israel'.

When is a Jew a Jew?

The word 'Jew' is used nowadays in two entirely different ways. Firstly, 'Jew' can be simply an ethnic or cultural term, referring to someone whose ancestry connects them with the Hebrew-speaking people of the ancient land of Israel. 'Jew', in this sense, is just like referring to someone as Anglo-Saxon or Celtic. You will therefore meet people today who insist they are Jews but have little or no interest in the religion we call Judaism.

Secondly, the word also has a *spiritual* usage. Jew, in this sense, means someone who follows the religion known as Judaism – they are devoted to the God of 'Israel'.

Which Israel?

That introduces another problem – the word 'Israel'. Today, 'Israel' usually means the State of Israel, that country founded in 1948 situated between Lebanon, Jordan, Egypt and the Mediterranean Sea. A similar political and geographical use of the term was popular in ancient times (say, 1000–100 BC), when the Land of Israel was ruled by Jewish monarchs such as King David (of 'David and Goliath' fame) and others.

Between the ancient Land of Israel and the founding of the modern State of Israel, the term 'Israel' meant far more than a piece of land in the Middle East. Israel was a collective reference to members of God's chosen people, the Jews, wherever they happened to live. Just as Christians speak of the universal 'church' and Muslims speak of the worldwide *umma* (Islamic community) so Jews, for most of their history, have referred to themselves as Israel.

The term 'Israel' throughout this section will usually be used in this collective spiritual sense. When I want to refer to the political or geographical 'Israel' I'll use phrases like the (ancient) 'Land of Israel' or the (modern) 'State of Israel'.

This may seem complicated or pedantic but, believe me, without clarifying these terms up front, our discussion of Judaism would get quite confusing. In short, all you have to remember is that 'Jew' in this book means *someone who follows the religion of Judaism* and 'Israel' means *the worldwide community of Jews*.

The four Judaisms of history

Our portrait of Judaism in the following chapters moves in four stages, roughly corresponding to four major periods in the history of Israel:

1. Foundational Judaism (2000–500 BC): when many of the fundamentals of the faith developed.

2. Interim Judaisms (500 BC–AD 100): when various factions among the Jewish people all competed for prominence.

3. Classical Judaism (AD 100–1800): when one form of Judaism emerged triumphant and set the course for the bulk of Jewish history.

4. Modern Judaisms (1800–present): when Classical Judaism evolved into the three versions of Jewish faith you might come across today.

Let's begin, then, with a look at Foundational Judaism.

13 Foundational Judaism

We begin with an overview of the origins of Israel as portrayed in their oldest Scriptures. As the Holocaust would illustrate for the twentieth century, the story of the Jews is a tale of great drama and endurance.

I should point out that historians often raise questions about the Jewish account of their origins as narrated in the biblical accounts (raising questions is what historians like to do). I don't want to completely ignore the insights of modern scholarship, but in what follows I intend to do what I have done in the previous sections: offer an account of origins that reflects the views of *traditional* believers – whether Hindu, Buddhist, or Jewish – not secular historians. Otherwise, this book would be about world history rather than world *religions*. In any case, what cannot be questioned is that these ancient traditions have ongoing significance in the lives of modern Jews, as the following explanation makes clear.

Circumcision and the family of Abraham

I said earlier that Hinduism pips Judaism at the post by about three centuries. This is because it is normal to speak about Judaism as beginning to take shape with the ancient figure of Moses (of 'Ten Commandments' fame) in the 1200s BC. Many Jews would dispute this, however, preferring to trace their origins 500 years earlier to the so-called 'patriarchs'.

According to the Jewish Scriptures, sometime around 1800 BC a man named Abram (also called Abraham), from a region in southern Iraq, was approached by the Creator and told to leave his country, his family, his culture and his pagan gods. In return, God would transform Abraham's descendants into a 'great nation' through which all nations in the world would be blessed (*Bereshit* 12:1–3, quoted on page 90). Abraham did the sensible thing and placed his destiny in the hands of the Almighty. In time his family would indeed begin to grow.

At this point, the biblical narrative introduces the rite of circumcision, the removal of the penis foreskin (or 'prepuce', for the technically minded). Abraham is told that every male in his family from that time on is to be circumcised as the sign of belonging to the chosen family. This 'mark' on the male reproductive organ was a perpetual reminder to the Jewish people that, whatever forces may work against them, God's people would multiply until they had reached their destiny.

To this day, the ritual of circumcision (*brit milah*) marks the beginning of Jewish life. On the eighth day of a Jewish boy's life, in the presence of at least ten Jewish men, a *mohel* (circumciser) performs the rite on the child with precision and expertise. Traditional blessings and prayers are said during the ceremony as the infant is welcomed into the promise of God and the world of Judaism.

Abraham's family began to grow. In fact, his grandson, Jacob, had twelve sons. This Jacob was also named 'Israel', which means *God strives* – God strives on behalf of his chosen people. The twelve sons of Jacob/Israel headed the twelve family clans, or tribes, of the Jewish people. The famous stage show *Joseph and the Amazing Technicolor Dream Coat* narrates the story of one of Jacob's sons, Joseph, who, after being sold into slavery by his brothers, ended up becoming a chief administrator in Egypt. This turned out rather well for the family of Israel, since it meant they could move to the safety of Egypt and avoid a famine that struck their own land. The family now numbered seventy people – not quite a 'nation' but a healthy-sized family nonetheless.

The importance of this sense of 'family' for Jews (ancient and modern) is difficult for many non-Jews, or Gentiles, to appreciate. Jews see themselves as part of an ancient, irrepressible and unique worldwide community of brothers and sisters – all descendants, whether by blood or by conversion, of Jacob/Israel. Circumcision, the mark of the covenant, underlines this point for Jews. What is sometimes perceived by Gentiles as 'exclusiveness' on the part of Jews is usually just the tell-tale signs of Israel's family connectedness.

Exodus and the Passover

Things were looking good for the original family of seventy living in Egypt in the eighteenth century BC. God's promise to Abraham seemed well on track. But then tragedy struck the family of Israel – the first of many in the course of their long history.

The Jewish Scriptures explain that the descendants of Abraham began to increase exponentially, so much so that after a few hundred years the 'family' of Israel numbered many thousands. Now they were a mini-nation within a nation.

Naturally, the Egyptians were not entirely happy with the expanding Israelite presence in their midst. Just as three millennia later Adolf Hitler would put Jews into slave camps, the Pharaohs of Egypt began to mistreat the descendants of Jacob, using them as a slave-nation to work on the massive building programmes of northern Egypt in the mid-1200s BC.

Enter Moses. Moses was a Jew with an Egyptian education and upbringing. His loyalty to the God of Israel, however, drove him passionately to seek the deliverance of his people, whom he daily witnessed being abused and even slaughtered. 'Let my people go,' was Moses' daring demand to Ramses II, the Pharaoh in charge of the world's No.1 Superpower. Not surprisingly, Ramses was unmoved.

At this point, the Jewish account describes a series of unspeakable disasters that fell upon Pharaoh and his kingdom: locust plagues, hail storms and, eventually, the mysterious death of Egyptian children.

This last tragedy convinces a reluctant Pharaoh to let Israel go. The day is commemorated in one of the most important festivals of the Jewish calendar, the Passover (more about that later). On that fateful evening God's judgment fell on the tyrannical Egyptians, but 'passed over' the Jews. Moses had instructed all the Israelites that night to kill, cook and eat a lamb, and to paint some of the blood of the animal on the outside doorframes of Jewish homes. In the words of *Shemot* 12:13:

> *The blood will be a sign for you on the houses where you are; and when I see the blood, I will pass over you. No destructive plague will touch you when I strike Egypt.*

Later that night the people of Israel were sent packing by their masters. Leaving the East Delta of Egypt, the Israelites escaped in their thousands across the *Yam Suph*, the Hebrew name for a lake or river of unknown location (sometimes called the Red Sea). The pursuing Egyptian squadron was drowned in the engulfing waters. The justice of God had fallen on the barbaric forces of Egypt (but had 'passed over' the Jews). The people of God were free to become the great nation promised to Abraham centuries before.

It is impossible to overstate the significance of the exodus for the Jewish faith (both then and now). In this event are contained many of the themes that saturate the Jewish consciousness – the oppression of Israel, God's love of Israel, and the eventual deliverance of Israel to become the 'great nation' pledged to the patriarchs. Even today Jews recall this exodus event as a microcosm of their entire history and as a symbol of their future: whatever troubles come upon Israel, the Lord of the universe will restore his chosen people to their rightful glory. God will *strive* for Israel.

The Torah and Jewish life

The next dramatic and important event in this potted account of traditional Jewish history is the provision of a national constitution, that is, laws by which the newly liberated people of God could be governed as they settle in the Promised Land (the Land of Israel).

To cut a long story short, a couple of months after leaving Egypt, Moses was called by God to go up a mountain somewhere in the Sinai Peninsula where he received, among other things, the famous Ten Commandments. It is probably unhelpful to focus on the Ten Commandments (even though it made for a classic Hollywood film) because the material revealed at Sinai far exceeds the themes covered in ten 'thou-shalt-nots'. Three entire books of the Jewish Scriptures (*Shemot* = Exodus; *Wayiqra* = Leviticus; *Devarim* = Deuteronomy) are devoted to outlining the contents of Israel's constitution as determined by God. Social welfare, criminal law, religious rituals, even environmental policy, all feature in the vast set of laws Jews call *Torah*.

'Torah' is an important word in Judaism so it requires an explanation. The word derives from the Hebrew for 'instruction' and, in the first instance, refers to God's *instruction* of the Israelites (at Sinai) in these legal, environmental, religious and social matters. From this usage the word Torah came to refer specifically to the first five books of the Jewish Bible in which these laws are narrated. The other two sections of the Jewish Bible are called Nevi'im (Prophets) and Ketuvim (Writings). The whole Jewish Bible, then, is often given the acronym TaNaK (Torah, Nevi'im, Ketuvim; or Law, Prophets, Writings). From this point on, I will frequently refer to the Jewish Bible (or what Christians call the Old Testament) as the *Tanak*.

Getting back to the word 'torah': because the second and third parts of the Tanak (the Prophets and the Writings) are heavily influenced by the first section (the Torah, or Law), the word 'Torah' came also to be used as a catch-all term for the whole 'instruction of God' revealed in all three sections of the Jewish Bible. Actually, Jews don't really use the word 'Bible'; they prefer 'Torah', either as a specific reference to the first section of the Scriptures, or as a broad reference to the entire Scriptures.

For now, it is worth simply remembering that Torah is an absolutely central concept in Judaism. It refers to the *instruction of God* revealed to Israel first through Moses and then through the entire sacred tradition of the Jews. What the 'Four Noble Truths' are to Buddhism, 'Torah' is to Judaism: pretty much everything.

The purpose of the Torah – God's instruction to the Jews-was to establish Israel as a divinely 'blessed people' through whom all other nations (*goyim* or 'Gentiles') would be blessed. The idea was quite simple. If God's people obeyed the social and ritual laws of the Torah, they would ensure the prosperity of their land, the security of their nationhood and the fulfilment of their divinely appointed role as a 'model' of wise and just society.

King David and the future Messiah

After the exodus from Egypt, the revelation of the Torah, and some time wandering around the desert, the newly freed people of Israel entered the Promised Land, where they encountered stiff resistance from the people who then occupied the land – the Canaanites. From around 1200 BC to around 1000 BC the nation of Israel was really a loose confederation of twelve not-very-peaceful family clans, each with its own patch of the land. What was needed, thought the Israelites, was leadership.

Enter King David (of David and Goliath fame). David was actually the *second* king of Israel but the first, Saul, was such a disaster we can skip over him with just a mention.

What do we know of King David? Well, for one thing, we know he was a frail human being like the rest of us. Two chapters of the Tanak describe a rather unflattering affair between David and the wife of one of his loyal military officers. The fact that the Tanak actually records this sin is extraordinary, given the tendency of ancient cultures to describe their favourite leaders in glowing terms.

More importantly, David was a great musician who wrote many religious songs; he was (and still is) known among Jews as the 'Sweet Singer of Israel'. The book of *Tehillim* (Psalms), part of the third section of the Tanak (the Writings), contains many hymns attributed to the king. One of them is introduced as the song of confession written after the affair just mentioned

(*Tehillim* 51). These songs of David are regularly used in Jewish prayers to this day.

Even more important than David's humanity and musical accomplishments is what he represented for Israel. This was the man who overthrew the pagan enemies of God, extended the borders of the land of Israel, and captured the holy city of Jerusalem. These events won David a central place in the hopes and dreams of traditional Jews from 1000 BC right up to today. According to a prophet of the time named Nathan, God had chosen David as the founder a kingdom and a dynasty that would last forever:

> *The Lord declares to you that the Lord himself will establish a*
> *house [i.e., dynasty] for you: When your days are over and you rest*
> *with your fathers, I will raise up your offspring to succeed you…*
> *and your kingdom will endure forever before me; your throne will*
> *be established forever (2 Samuel 7:11–16).*

The interesting thing here is that this divine promise extends far beyond the time of David (tenth century BC): the throne of David described here would be 'established forever'.

The importance of the figure of King David for Judaism is difficult to overstate. The promise that David's kingdom would be 'established forever' is the basis for the enduring Jewish belief in a future 'Messiah'. The word 'Messiah' ('Christ' is the Greek equivalent) is Hebrew for 'anointed one', a reference to the anointing ceremony (or coronation) in which oil was poured over the king as a symbol of divine power and blessing. David was anointed in just this way. According to numerous prophecies in the Tanak, a future son of David would be the Anointed One in an ultimate sense.

Later Jewish teachers (AD 100–200) would go on to explain the conditions under which the kingdom of the Messiah, God's kingdom, would come. They argued that the central issue in determining when the Messiah would come was Israel's *obedience* to the Torah. Meticulous personal purity and complete community commitment to God's instruction would usher in the long-awaited messianic kingdom.

One fixed prayer, said almost daily by traditional Jews for almost 2,000 years, reveals just how fervent is the longing for the promised descendant of King David:

> *The offspring of Your servant David may You speedily cause to flourish, and enhance his pride through Your salvation, for we hope for Your salvation all day long* (Shemoneh Esrei 15).

Again, the traditional prayer said by Jews after each weekday meal pleads:

> *Have mercy Lord, our God, on Israel Your people; on Jerusalem, Your city, on Zion (the hill on which Jerusalem was built), the resting place of Your Glory; on the monarchy of the house of David, your Messiah* (Rahem, *Third Blessing After Meals*).

The memory of King David, and his rule on God's behalf, established forever in Jewish thought the hope of an eternal king (the Messiah) by whose reign Israel would achieve its purpose.

Temple, forgiveness and worship

David's successor and son, King Solomon, built one of the most important features of Israel's religion, a feature comparable in importance to the Torah and the King. I am speaking about the great *temple* of God in the holy city of Jerusalem.

The temple built by Solomon was not an enormous structure – about the size of a large church building today – but its significance in Jewish life was immense. The temple represented the throne-room of God, a kind of 'palace' for the Universal King. Jews knew that God was located everywhere in the universe but they also believed men and women could approach the omnipresent King in a tangible way in the Jerusalem temple, just as earthly subjects might humbly approach a king in his royal court.

A huge number of priests was employed to run the temple functions. Key among their tasks was offering sacrifices to

God. Some of these were animal sacrifices, offered to God on huge burning altars in the heart of the temple. The priests often ate the cooked portions of these animals. Other daily sacrifices included simple offerings of grain and bread. Much of this also was consumed by the priests.

The purpose of the offerings depended on the particular ritual used. Sometimes offerings were expressions of thanks to God – people would bring some of their harvest and ask the priests to dedicate it to God as a 'thank you'. Other sacrifices symbolized the forgiveness of sins. If a member of Israel had committed some act of disobedience to the Torah, he or she could take an animal to the temple and have it sacrificed as a picture of God's judgment falling on the animal instead of the 'sinner'. This 'atonement' concept is central to Jewish thought.

Perhaps the most important temple sacrifice took place just once a year, on the Day of Atonement, or *Yom Kippur*. It was a festival celebrating the mercy of God toward the whole of Israel. Two goats were presented to the high priest. One would be slaughtered and its blood sprinkled on the central altar in the Most Holy Place in the temple. The picture here was again of God's judgment falling on the animal instead of the people of Israel. The other goat had a more pleasant fate and provided a wonderful picture of divine forgiveness. The priest would lay both hands on the live goat's head while confessing to God the many sins of Israel. Then, in the company of someone appointed for the task, the goat would be led out into the wilderness of southern Israel and released. This was a potent symbol of Israel's sins being removed from God's presence, never to be thought of again. We get the expression 'scapegoat' (someone who takes the blame for another) from this ancient *Yom Kippur* ceremony.

The temple with its large courtyard also provided a venue for singing and learning. People would regularly gather in the courtyard to sing their praises to God, accompanied by a large band of musicians playing strings, horns and percussion.

While assembled, people would listen to the priests and other learned sages who would expound the Torah and urge people to remain faithful to the God who had delivered them from Egypt. The faithful would respond with prayers of thanksgiving, confession and devotion. The temple was also a place of counsel. People would come to a priest seeking personal instruction, direction and blessing for the needs of daily life.

One cannot overstate the central place of the Jerusalem temple in ancient Jewish life – and in modern Jewish imagination – but a mere three centuries after the reign of King Solomon that glorious structure would lie in ruins. Here we arrive at the second great disaster in Jewish history.

Destruction of the first temple (586 BC)

The Tanak is a bizarre document in many ways. Most national histories – such as those of the Egyptians or, later, the Greeks – tend to play down the nation's failures. The sacred history of the Jews is different. According to the biblical books that narrate the period after King Solomon, the Jews did not obey the Torah. Justice was perverted, other gods were worshipped and violence abounded, even among the kings and priests of Israel whose task it was to keep the rest of Israel on track.

God sent 'prophets' during these centuries, says the Tanak, many of whose writings are now contained in the second portion of the Jewish Scriptures (the Nevi'im, or Prophets). These charismatic leaders pleaded with kings and commoners alike to return to the Torah, to obey the God who had rescued them from Egypt, who had promised them an eternal kingdom, and who had granted them the temple with its rituals of forgiveness. The people rejected the prophets and in some cases killed them.

But the warnings of the prophets proved true – which is probably partly why their writings were revered and preserved. These divine heralds predicted that if Israel did not turn back to the way of the Torah, God would allow foreign nations to invade the land, destroy the temple, and 'export' the Jews into foreign lands where they would again, as in Egypt centuries before, become a slave nation.

Sure enough, in the mid- to late 700s BC the kingdom of Assyria, under kings with such fancy names as Tiglath-pileser III, Shalmaneser V and Sargon II, conquered the northern part of the land of Israel. Then, 150 years later King Nebuchadrezzar II (sometimes spelt Nebuchadnezzar) of Babylon (modern Iraq) moved his armies into the southern part of the land of Israel and in 586 BC did exactly as the prophets had warned: he destroyed the temple and carried off into exile (in Babylon) many of the wealthiest and best-educated members of Jewish society. Israel was now a ghost of what it had once been.

But the prophets of this period also predicted a brighter future for Israel. After a time of judgment, they insisted, God would again restore the fortunes of his people. The temple would be rebuilt, the exiles would return to the land, and Israel would finally become a 'great nation' through which all nations would be 'blessed'.

Things *sort of* panned out as the prophets described. Less than fifty years after the sacking of Jerusalem, there was a new superpower on the block, Cyrus II of Persia (modern Iran) who, after defeating Babylon, issued a decree in 538 BC that the Jews should return to their land and rebuild their temple. That is exactly what many Jews did and, less than twenty-five years later, the temple with its sacred rituals and public worship of God was back in use. The prophets' predictions had come true – almost.

14 Interim Judaisms

So far, we have been discussing what I have called Foundational Judaism. Without question, much of what first emerged in that era still determines Jewish belief and practice. The importance of belonging to Abraham's family, circumcision, obedience to the laws of the Torah, veneration of the Tanak as God's word, celebration of the festivals of Passover, Day of Atonement, hope for an eternal messianic kingdom, and so on – all of these are found in Judaism today.

And yet, significant changes also took place in Judaism after this foundational period. The dramas of the Jewish people would go from bad to worse, and Jews would respond to these events in a number of different, somewhat contradictory, ways. These different responses are what I am calling Interim Judaisms, that is, the versions of Judaism that existed temporarily before 'Classical Judaism' (discussed in the next chapter) emerged victorious in the second century AD.

The dramas of the second temple

The second temple (referred to earlier) received numerous renovations in the centuries after it was built. Actually, in the late first century BC the temple area was expanded to roughly the size of a modern football stadium. It became a cause of great cultural pride for the Jews.

After the Persians (sixth–fourth centuries BC) came the Hellenistic (or Greek) empire, under Alexander the Great and his successors (fourth–second centuries BC). These Hellenistic kings ruled the Jews with a leadership style ranging from indifferent to outright tyrannical. One of the worst was Antiochus IV Epiphanes, who slaughtered thousands of Jews and in 167 BC had the audacity to set up in the Jewish temple an idol to the pagan god Zeus Olympios. Nothing could have been more heartbreaking and offensive to ancient Jews.

These events sparked a Jewish rebellion which, quite amazingly, resulted in a victory for the Jews under the leadership of one Judas Maccabeus, a brilliant army general from a priestly family. Judas quickly restored Jewish worship and rededicated the temple to the one true God (164 BC). This event is still celebrated today in the Jewish *Hanukkah* ('Dedication') festival, which occurs around Christmas time (more about this later).

Just as importantly, Judas Maccabeus founded a century-long dynasty of Jewish priest-kings who ruled Jerusalem and its environs as a free and autonomous state. Was this the beginning of the glorious future predicted by the Prophets? Unfortunately not.

The Hasmonean Dynasty (as the Maccabean kings were called) came to an end in 63 BC. The Romans had arrived, and most things gave way when the Romans came to town! The entry of the Romans into Palestine (the Roman name for the Land of Israel) marked the end of a free Jewish state. Not until 1948 – 2,000 years later – would the Jews have any jurisdiction over the 'Promised Land'.

Heavy taxes were imposed by the Romans and a strong military presence was felt throughout the region. Numerous Jewish uprisings were of little consequence and, when the Jews started an all-out war against their occupiers (AD 66–70), Rome responded with devastating force. The people of Jerusalem were massacred, and the temple of God was brought to the ground a second time (on 29 August AD 70). What was once the centre of Jewish religious life was now a mound of rubble.

Jews as a people of hope

All that remains of the second temple today is a 50-metre (164-foot) section of the western wall, often called the 'Wailing Wall', where modern Jews cry out to God for the restoration of his temple. Unfortunately (from the Jewish point of view), standing where the temple once stood is the Dome of the Rock, the oldest Islamic monument in the world (built around AD 690). It is the world's most hotly disputed piece of real estate!

The final destruction of the temple was not the end as far as the Jews were concerned. They still had the Prophets, those sacred writings that promised not only disaster for Israel but, one day, great glory. And here is the important point for now: if the Torah provides Jews with the *instruction* for living here and now, the Prophets provide Jews with a *hope* for the future. Perhaps no group in the history of the world has suffered as profoundly as the Jews. Yet, Israel remains expectant: the promise to Abraham will be fulfilled; the deliverance of the exodus will be repeated; the prophecies of a new temple and an eternal messianic kingdom will be realized.

In the hotbed of drama that was ancient Palestine it is not surprising that Jews responded to the crises and victories (and further crises) by proposing different visions of what Israel should be and do. Scholars often point to at least five different Judaisms in this 'interim' period. Four of them will be discussed in the remainder of this chapter. The fifth ushered in Classical Judaism and so will be treated separately in the following chapter.

Sadducees: aristocrats and priests

The first faction of Judaism in this period was the Sadducees, a group of conservative Jews who rejected innovations in the faith, especially ones that might diminish the role of priest and temple. Sadducees appear to have dominated the priesthood and formed a kind of religious aristocracy in Jerusalem.

When the Romans came to power in Palestine (63 BC) those who remained loyal to Rome were able to keep their positions in Jewish society. The Sadducees largely cooperated with the invaders and were thus able to assert their influence in the holy city and bolster their temple-focused vision of Judaism.

Essenes: apocalyptic holy men

But not everyone was happy with the power and wealth of the Jerusalem elite. Our second 'faction' in this period was the Essenes. You may have heard of the so-called Dead Sea Scrolls, a huge collection of writings found in 1947 in caves around Qumran on the north-western shore of the Dead Sea (southern Israel).

The Scrolls are believed by most scholars to have been produced by the Essenes, a group of ultra-devout Jews who avoided the 'impure' cities of Israel and lived in self-sufficient communities where they shared their possessions, studied the Torah, and engaged in meticulous bathing and eating rituals.

Zealots: fighters and patriots

Another vision of Israel was promoted by a third faction, the Zealots. As you might work out from their name, the Zealots were fiercely loyal to the traditions of Judaism and violently opposed to the Roman presence in the holy land. Whereas the Sadducees opted for cooperation with the Imperial powers, and the Essenes chose to remove themselves from public life, the Zealots decided to fight. They staged various uprisings climaxing in a reign of terror around AD 60–70 in which they resorted to assassinating key Jewish leaders who they believed were collaborating with Rome. The Zealot assassins were known as *Sicarii* ('dagger men'): they would move about the crowded streets of Jerusalem, with knives concealed under their clothing, before murdering their victims and slipping away undetected. Extreme times called for extreme measures.

Followers of Yeshua: heretics of a false Messiah

A fourth faction of first-century Judaism was launched by a man named Yeshua ben Yosef, or the more anglicized 'Jesus son of Joseph'. A simple peasant from northern Palestine, Yeshua explicitly rejected the aims of the Zealots. He demanded that his fellow Jews 'turn the other cheek' and love their enemies (which included the Romans).

Some hailed Yeshua as a healer and a prophet. Others denounced him as a magician and deceiver. The Sadducees, in particular, were deeply troubled by the man. Not only was it rumoured that he presumed to hand out God's forgiveness (historically, the core business of the temple), but some began to suppose this man might be the long-awaited Son of David, the Messiah. This threatened to upset the good relations the Sadducees had fostered with the Romans.

Yeshua was removed, and crucified outside Jerusalem during the Passover festival of AD 30. His followers, however, preserved his memory and promoted his teachings, first in the land of Israel, then throughout all the lands of the Roman Empire and beyond. The movement became known as Christianity.

By the beginning of the second century, a generation after the destruction of the temple, Christianity would no longer be considered a faction within Israel; rather, it would be seen as a perversion of Israel's faith. This was partly due to the success of yet another version of Judaism, one that would declare the followers of Yeshua to be *minim*, or 'heretics'.

This fifth type of Judaism would offer a comprehensive vision of what it meant to be a Jew when the temple lay in ruins. It is a vision that would set the course of Judaism for the next two millennia. This fifth stream, therefore, cannot be described as an *interim* Judaism. It began with a group known as the Pharisees and emerged into what is known as Classical Judaism.

15 Classical Judaism

In discussing the rise of Classical Judaism I don't want to give the impression that this form of the faith was a radical break with what went before. It was not. All of the aspects discussed earlier in our study of Judaism – the sense of family, circumcision, the importance of the exodus, the laws of the Torah, the religious festivals, the hope of the Prophets, and so on – featured prominently in Classical Judaism.

Classical Judaism began with a group known as the Pharisees.

The Pharisees, the temple and the synagogues

In the period of the 'priest-kings' of Israel (164–63 BC) a group arose in Israel that stressed the need for *personal* purity in the affairs of ordinary life. The group consisted of both scholars and ordinary believers (and included some priests as well). It was more a reform movement than a political party. Members of the movement came to be called 'Pharisees', probably from the Hebrew word *parush*, meaning 'separated', that is, separated from impure things.

In emphasizing individual purity, the Pharisees developed intricate rules concerning the affairs of daily existence – how you ate, how you washed, how and when you worked, with whom you could associate, how much of your possessions to give to God, and so on. These laws came to be known as the 'traditions of the elders' because they had been passed down from generation to generation. These traditions were sacred and were designed to promote total obedience to the Torah revealed to Moses at Sinai.

While the temple was still standing Pharisees were simply a parallel movement in Jewish life, sometimes prominent, sometimes peripheral. However, when that temple was destroyed in AD 70, never to be rebuilt, conditions were perfect for Pharisaic teachers, called *rabbis*, to capture the public imagination.

These rabbis had always said that what counted most in life was personal devotion to the Torah (and the 'traditions of the elders'). Now, with the temple gone, this emphasis seemed the most sensible option.

The success of the Pharisees was no doubt assisted by the emergence (some time between 500 and 200 BC) of the synagogue, the Jewish equivalent of 'church'. Admittedly, this is a strange way to describe this Jewish institution since the Christian idea of 'church' derived from the Jewish idea of 'synagogue'. In any case, the synagogue was an official gathering of Jews (ten males at a minimum) who met together, usually in a purpose-built space, to pray, to hear the Torah, to sing, and to study. It provided a context in which Jews could express their faith in an organized way outside of the Jerusalem temple. And, if you lived a long way from the holy city, this was a 'godsend'.

For the Pharisees, then, the synagogue was the perfect venue from which to teach the masses the importance of the 'traditions of the elders'. When the temple in Jerusalem was destroyed, and the role of the priests was thereby diminished, the synagogues became indispensable and the role of the Pharisees pivotal.

The result of all this, early in the second century AD, was the triumph of the Judaism of the Pharisees (sometimes also called 'Rabbinic Judaism'). All Judaisms, from that time on, owe their existence to this classical form of the faith.

The rise of the 'dual-Torah'

Let me now try to describe something of the comprehensive vision of (post-temple) Jewish life that was offered by the Pharisees and that was crystallized in Classical Judaism. We begin with perhaps the most significant aspect of that vision, the insistence that the Torah given to Moses was two-fold.

After the destruction of the temple in Jerusalem many rabbis fled the holy city to establish communities devoted to the study of the Torah and the 'traditions of the elders'. The most famous of these was at Jamnia (near the south coast of Palestine). There rabbis were required to learn and memorize not only the written Tanak but also the insights and rulings of their rabbinic predecessors. In fact, these ever-growing 'traditions of the elders' were regarded by Rabbinic Judaism as part of the Torah itself, part of the instruction of God revealed to Moses.

Here is a critical point in the development of Judaism: these rabbis said that the Torah is *two*-fold. When God spoke to Moses at Sinai in the 1200s BC only *part* of that revelation was written down. The other part was passed on 'orally', that is, by word of mouth, first to Joshua (Moses' assistant), then on to the subsequent generations, right up to the Pharisees of the post-temple period. The 'traditions of the elders', therefore, are not simply man-made rules as some had claimed (Yeshua ben Yosef, for instance); they are the very instruction of God. At this point, then, we must meet the second holy book of Classical Judaism, the *Mishnah*.

The Mishnah

Somewhere around AD 200 the leader of the Jews of Palestine, Rabbi Judah ha-Nasi, decided to bring into one volume all of the 'traditions of the elders' as they were preserved in the memories of his fellow rabbis. As in the Buddhist tradition, (see chapter 9) it is important to remember that sacred (and secular) teachings in the ancient world were usually committed to memory and then very strictly passed on to others who, in turn, would be able accurately to pass on the traditions to others. Scholars regard the ancient process of *oral tradition* as a highly effective (though, of course, not foolproof) means of transmitting information. The end result of Rabbi Judah ha-Nasi's collection of oral material was a single volume known as the Mishnah, which means 'repetition' – repetition, of course, was the principal means of memorizing and passing on the traditions.

The Mishnah records the 'sayings' and 'legal opinions' of about 150 rabbis from the first and second centuries AD. Their statements, however, are believed to preserve the instruction given to Moses 1,300 years before. The opening paragraph of one very popular chapter in the Mishnah explains:

> Moses received the Torah [i.e., the oral Torah] from Sinai and transmitted it to Joshua; Joshua to the elders; the elders to the prophets; and the prophets handed it down to the men of the Great Assembly [a gathering in the 4th/5th century BC]. They said three things: Be deliberate in judgment, raise up many disciples, and make a fence around the Torah (Mishnah, Sayings of the Fathers, Avot 1).

The Mishnah has sixty-three chapters (usually called 'tractates') in six topical divisions: (1) agricultural rules; (2) laws about 'appointed times', that is, religious festivals and the like; (3) commands relating to women (marriage and divorce); (4) rulings about legal damages; (5) regulations about the Jerusalem temple; (6) decrees on 'purity' (food laws, bathing rituals, handling of animals and so on). My copy of the Mishnah runs to over 1,100 pages. That's a lot of instruction.

In Classical Judaism the Mishnah is a holy book on par with the Tanak. Both documents record God's 'instruction' of his people, Israel. Hence, the Tanak and the Mishnah, together, are called the dual-Torah.

Two other sets of holy books exist in Classical Judaism, and are still revered today.

Midrash and the Talmud

The first set of documents is called Midrash, from the Hebrew word for 'investigation'. Midrash is a vast body of works devoted to interpreting sections of the Tanak. Very ancient biblical texts are thus recast to have contemporary significance.

Just as Midrash interprets the Tanak, so another set of books interprets the Mishnah. This is called the Talmud, meaning 'study' or 'learning', and there are two of them. One Talmud was compiled in the holy land around AD 400 and is called the Palestinian Talmud. The other was compiled in Babylon around AD 600 and is called, not surprisingly, the Babylonian Talmud.

The Judaism of the dual-Torah (written and oral) set the course of the Jewish faith for centuries (and, for many, even today). Let me now unpack some of the most important features of this Classical Judaism.

Five annual festivals of Classical Judaism

One of the most enduring legacies of Classical Judaism is the fixed Jewish calendar with its festivals of joy and sorrow. Although festivals had always been a part of Judaism, the rabbis of the Mishnah and Talmud set down in detail many of the guidelines for how these celebrations should be conducted.

There are five main festivals in the Jewish calendar, each designed to recall some aspect of the Jewish vision of God and the world.

1. *New Year (Rosh Hashanah)*. The Jewish New Year begins with the appearance of the new moon in the month of Tishri (September–October). Far from being an occasion of excitement and joy (as are New Year's celebrations in Western culture), Rosh Hashanah is a sombre day. Israel is reminded by this festival of its important duties as the people of God.

New Year begins a ten-day period of soul-searching in which Jews assess their relationship with God and with one another. The synagogue service for the Rosh Hashanah festival features the sounding of the ram's horn, the *shofar*, as a call to spiritual awakening.

2. *Day of Atonement (Yom Kippur)*. Ten days after New Year the period of self-examination climaxes in the Day of the Atonement, or Yom Kippur (10th of Tishri). In the chapter on Foundational Judaism we saw that this day symbolized God's forgiveness of his people.

While sacrifices are no longer made on Yom Kippur – these were only ever conducted in the temple – the day still commemorates God's mercy. It is marked by prayer, confession of sin, abstaining from food, drink and sex, and a synagogue service that goes from morning until evening, just as the rabbis of the Mishnah and Talmud instructed.

3. *Feast of Tabernacles (Sukkot)*. Five days after Yom Kippur comes the Feast of Tabernacles (Tishri is quite a month), which commemorates the period when Israel wandered in the wilderness of Sinai (just after receiving the Torah) and lived in makeshift tents or 'tabernacles'.

Lasting for eight days, the most striking part of the festivities is the construction of frail huts (recalling the ancient tabernacles). The faithful sit in these to eat their meals.

4. *Passover (Pessah)*. Several months after the Feast of Tabernacles comes the great Passover festival. On the evening of the 14th of Nisan (around March–April), Jews begin a week-long celebration of God's rescue of his people from Egypt. The meal on the eve of the festival (which is often repeated the next night) is called the seder. It is quite an elaborate affair. Following a special service at the synagogue, families gather to eat special foods, each with its own spiritual significance: lamb to recall the sacrifice of the first Passover animal; bitter herbs to remember the suffering of Egypt; bread without leaven in imitation of the first Israelites, who fled Egypt without time to bake leavened bread; and wine to mark the freedom and joy of God's deliverance. Various traditional prayers and blessings are said during the meal. The Passover festival is also called the Feast of Unleavened Bread.

5. *Feast of Weeks (Shavuot)*. Fifty days after Passover the Feast of Weeks celebrates the giving of the law at Sinai.

Also called Pentecost (Greek for 'fiftieth Day'), the Feast of Weeks is marked by special synagogue services at which portions of the Tanak are read. In addition, many Jews spend the whole night reading and studying the Torah, reminding themselves of the great gift of God's instruction. Many Jewish schools and colleges hold their graduations on this day.

Other Holy Days

1. *Sabbath (Shabbat)*. Just as the five major festivals mark the cycle of the *year* so the Sabbath marks the cycle of the *week*. The fourth commandment of the well-known Ten Commandments states:

> *Remember the Sabbath day by keeping it holy. Six days you shall labor and do all your work, but the seventh day is a Sabbath to the Lord your God (*Shemot 19:8*).*

The Sabbath officially commences at sunset on Friday evening and concludes at sunset on Saturday evening. More precisely, the classical rabbis declared that the Sabbath finishes when at least three stars are visible in the Saturday night sky.

No work is conducted by Jews on the Sabbath and, again, the ancient rabbis stipulated with great care what constitutes 'work'. But Sabbath is far more than a simple 'day off'. It is a time for Jews to attend the synagogue with other believers (up to three times in twenty-four hours), to eat special meals with family members, to say prayers, to light candles and, of course, to study the Torah.

2. *Bar/bat Mitzvah*. The Torah is honoured in another ceremony which marks a teenager's transition into Jewish adulthood.

The rabbis of the classical period declared that thirteen was the age at which Jewish boys could understand and obey the dual-Torah. Based on this ruling a ceremony was devised to celebrate the moment. The *bar mitzvah* ('son of commandment') is a simple ritual. The boy (usually aged thirteen) is called to the front of the synagogue where the Tanak is found. He then reads aloud two set passages, one from the Law, the other from the Prophets. Prayers are said, wine is shared, and a family meal is usually enjoyed.

A female version of the *bar mitzvah* is practised in many synagogues today. It is called the *bat mitzvah* ('daughter of commandment').

3. *Hanukkah.* The final festival mentioned here rose to prominence in the Jewish community only recently – perhaps as a healthy competitor to the Christmas season (both fall in December).

As mentioned previously, Hanukkah means 'dedication', and the Hanukkah festival commemorates the rededication of the temple by Judas Maccabeus (164 BC) after the Hellenistic ruler Antiochus IV Epiphanes had desecrated the temple by placing a pagan idol in it. Candles are lit for eight days during the modern festival because, according to the rabbis of the Talmud, when Judas Maccabeus relit the sacred oil of the temple lamps, a single day's oil miraculously lasted eight days.

Prayers of Classical Judaism

Any presentation of Classical Judaism would be incomplete without some discussion of the prayers set down by the rabbis of the post-temple period. These sages were not simply legislators of legal and ritual matters; they were deeply religious men with a particular vision of the nature and destiny of Israel. The prayers they devised, which are now found in the Siddur, or Jewish prayer book, continue to exert enormous influence over synagogues and individuals today.

1. *The Shema.* Nothing is more basic to Jewish prayer than a simple, three-line statement called the *Shema* ('hear'). Traditionally, every Jew is obliged to say the *Shema* in the morning and in the evening. So important is this brief affirmation that the Mishnah treats the *Shema* as its first topic, setting out in great detail when and how the prayer should be performed. According to the rabbis, various introductory blessings are to be said in the 'build up' to the *Shema*: these prepare those praying for the central affirmation that follows.

Then, with full concentration on the majesty of God, the faithful declare:

Hear (shema), O Israel: The Lord is our God, the Lord, the One and Only (Shema from Devarim *[= Deuteronomy] 6:4).*

In this statement, the Jew proclaims that there is one God who has set his affection on one people, Israel. Then follows immediately a statement about what it means to be the people of the One and Only God:

You shall love the Lord, your God, with all your heart, with all your soul and with all your resources. Let these matters that I command you today be upon your heart. Teach them thoroughly to your children and speak of them while you sit in your home, while you walk on the way, when you retire and when you arise (from Devarim *[= Deuteronomy] 6:5–7).*

The importance of God's instruction is emphasized here, reminding the Jew that the chief sign of God's love for Israel is his revelation of the Torah and that the chief sign of Israel's love for God is devotion to these commands.

2. The Eighteen Prayers (Shemoneh Esrei or Amidah). A generation after the fall of Jerusalem (in AD 70) the great rabbinical 'university' at Jamnia produced a leader whose contribution to the prayer life of the Jews is made clear every day of the Jewish year. Rabbi Gamaliel II (2nd century AD) brought great unity to the Jews by collecting and revising a set of eighteen fixed prayers (*Shemoneh Esrei* = 'Eighteen'). These, like the *Shema*, are meant to be said by every Jew every day – though, on the Sabbath only about half are said. A nineteenth prayer was added by Gamaliel to denounce the *minim*, or 'heretics'. Among the heretics included here were the followers of Yeshua (Christian Jews). The set of prayers is also called the *Amidah* ('standing') because of the position in which you are to say them. In terms of importance, the *Amidah* (with the *Shema*) is to Jews what the 'Lord's Prayer' (or 'Our Father') is to Christians.

Several major themes of Judaism are captured in the statements of the *Amidah* – membership in Abraham's family, confidence in the afterlife (resurrection from the dead), confession of sin, hope for the Messiah, denunciation of heretics, and so on. A petition for the restoration of Jerusalem also features:

> *And to Jerusalem, Your city, may You return in compassion, and may You rest within it, as You have spoken. May You rebuild it soon in our days as an eternal structure (* Shemoneh Esrei *14).*

Nothing reveals the heart of a people more than their prayers, and the *Shemoneh Esrei* (or *Amidah*) and the *Shema* do this particularly well for the Jewish people. Although composed more than 1,800 years ago, these Jewish prayers still exercise enormous power in the life of traditional Jews.

The thirteen principles of faith

The five major festivals, together with the *Shema* and the Eighteen Prayers, provide a good summary of Jewish 'liturgical' (worship) life. What about beliefs? Where can we find a succinct summary of the principles held dear by Classical Judaism (and, for the most part, modern Judaisms)? The so-called Thirteen Principles of Faith were composed in the twelfth century by the great Jewish scholar Moses Maimonides, also known as Rambam. These thirteen statements take us to the heart of Judaism and are part of the weekday synagogue service to this day. They are worth quoting in full:

> *1. I believe with perfect faith that God is the Creator and Ruler of all things. He alone has made, does make, and will make all things.*
> *2. I believe with perfect faith that God is One. There is no unity that is in any way like His. He alone is our God He was, He is, and He will be.*
> *3. I believe with perfect faith that God does not have a body. Physical concepts do not apply to Him. There is nothing whatsoever that resembles Him at all.*

4. I believe with perfect faith that God is first and last.
5. I believe with perfect faith that it is only proper to pray to God. One may not pray to anyone or anything else.
6. I believe with perfect faith that all the words of the prophets are true.
7. I believe with perfect faith that the prophecy of Moses is absolutely true. He was the chief of all prophets, both before and after Him.
8. I believe with perfect faith that the entire Torah that we now have is that which was given to Moses.
9. I believe with perfect faith that this Torah will not be changed, and that there will never be another given by God.
10. I believe with perfect faith that God knows all of man's deeds and thoughts. It is thus written (Psalm 33:15), 'He has molded every heart together, He understands what each one does.'
11. I believe with perfect faith that God rewards those who keep His commandments, and punishes those who transgress Him.
12. I believe with perfect faith in the coming of the Messiah. How long it takes, I will await His coming every day.
*13. I believe with perfect faith that the dead will be brought back to life when God wills it to happen (*Siddur, *from the* Shacharis, *or Weekday Morning Service).*

In emphasizing these shared beliefs, prayers and festivals of Judaism, it has to be pointed out that not everyone in Israel still abides by the traditions of the classical rabbis. The following chapter explains why.

16 Modern Judaisms

I've said several times that Classical Judaism reigned supreme in the Jewish faith for most of the last two millennia. Wherever the Jews lived – and they lived in lots of places – the vision of Israel cast by these ancient classical rabbis dominated the outlook of Jewish existence. This began to change, however, in the eighteenth and nineteenth centuries.

The 'emancipation' of the Jews

Sadly, for most of the period of Classical Judaism, Jews lived as a tolerated but excluded minority, firstly under pagan Rome, then under Christian and Islamic rule. In some ways, Classical Judaism coped well with this, since *separation* from an impure world was a core part of the Jewish mindset in that period. Jews stuck to their own districts, dressed in their own way, ate their own food, managed their own communities, conducted their own rituals and worked at their own professions and trades. Integration with the wider world just wasn't on the agenda.

Then came 'emancipation', a Europe-wide movement in the late 1700s and early 1800s that sought to bring rights and freedoms to oppressed minorities – to women, to Catholics (in Protestant countries), to slaves, and to Jews.

For the first time in centuries, Israel was invited to enter into wider society. This raised a fundamental question for the Jew: to what extent can I integrate into the non-Jewish world and still be part of God's holy people? Put another way: can I be both a member of Israel and a good citizen of Germany, France, the United States or wherever? Jews in the 1800s answered this question – the question of integration – in three divergent ways. These different answers led to the emergence of three distinct Judaisms.

Reform Judaism: the way of integration

In the early 1800s a German layman named Israel Jacobson began to make small changes to the synagogue service. These were mainly designed to make the synagogue more accessible and inviting to his fellow Jews. The prayers and ceremonies were made shorter, choirs were introduced, services were conducted in German instead of Hebrew (which few people understood), and men and women were allowed to sit together in the synagogue. Jacobson's changes soon spread throughout Europe and the United States.

This interest in changing the form of Jewish ceremonies soon evolved into a desire to change the substance of Jewish belief. Those making the changes had no intention of overthrowing Judaism; rather, they hoped to *reform* Israel, making it more suitable for the new situation confronting Jews. This movement became known as Reform Judaism, complete with its own synagogues and rabbinical training schools.

What was new about Reform belief and practice? Firstly, perhaps the greatest change was the rejection of the oral Torah. Reform Jews regard the Tanak as God's instruction but consider the Mishnah and Talmud to be simply human wisdom that can be discarded to suit changing times.

Secondly, Reform Judaism does not look forward to, or pray for, the revived Jerusalem temple, the coming of an individual Messiah and the future resurrection of the dead. This means that the parts of the Eighteen/Nineteen Prayers (the *Shemoneh Esrei*, or *Amidah*) which mention these things were revised in the Reform prayer book.

Thirdly, the intricate food laws and Sabbath rules of Foundational and Classical Judaism are considered by Reform Judaism to be too restrictive in a modern context, and so are declared obsolete. The same applies, fourthly, to some biblical moral laws. Homosexuality, for instance, is regarded by Reform Judaism as permissible.

Reform is the dominant form of Judaism today, especially in the United States, and is sometimes also called Progressive Judaism.

Orthodox Judaism: the way of separation

Not everyone was happy with the reforms of Reform Judaism. By the middle of the 1800s many denounced Reform as 'apostasy', an abandonment of Israel's true faith. This reaction led to the establishment of what is called Orthodox Judaism. The word 'orthodox' comes from the Greek 'of right opinion', so it is easy to understand how such Jews perceive themselves. They insist that they are the keepers of the historic (Classical) Jewish faith. They claim that their opinions conform to God's instruction revealed in the dual-Torah. Obviously, then, Orthodox Judaism reveres the Tanak, the Mishnah and the Talmud. In this way, Orthodox Judaism and Classical Judaism would appear virtually identical.

Orthodox Jews adhere strictly to the rulings of the ancient rabbis concerning the handling of food, ritual washings, Sabbath keeping, the festivals, and so on. They also conduct synagogue services in Hebrew and prohibit the use of musical instruments in public worship. Deep integration into the politics of society is rejected. Jews are the chosen people and must keep themselves 'clean'.

Having said this, there are actually *two* types of Orthodox Judaism, one which completely rejects integration with society and one which, while living by the dual-Torah, does allow *some* integration into Gentile culture. This second stream of Orthodox Judaism does not insist, for example, on the wearing of distinctive Jewish clothing. It also permits Jews to conduct business with Gentiles and, significantly, to attend non-Jewish schools and universities.

Orthodox Judaism is prominent in South Africa, Australia and Europe. It is also the official form of Judaism in the modern State of Israel.

Conservative Judaism: the way of compromise

Disappointed with the integrationist approach of Reform Judaism, and wary of the separationist approach of the Orthodox, a so-called 'middle' position emerged in Judaism around 1850. It is called Conservative Judaism.

Conservative Jews, like the Orthodox, maintain the food laws, Sabbath rules, all the major festivals, belief in the Messiah, and commitment to preserving the Hebrew language. They also revere the Mishnah and Talmud (the oral Torah).

Conservative Jews part company with the Orthodox in believing that the sacred texts of the oral Torah must be subject to historical analysis. This analysis, in their view, reveals which teachings of the ancient rabbis are peripheral (and therefore changeable) and which are central (and therefore unchangeable). Conservative Judaism, for instance, has allowed women to become rabbis for almost twenty years, something not countenanced in the Mishnah or Talmud. Conservatives tend to be less flexible with the teachings of the Tanak (the written Torah).

Perhaps the best way to think about this 'middle' position in Judaism is to see it as conservative in *practice* (its rituals and morals) but flexible in its *thinking*. One Jewish scholar I read recently described the Conservative stance as: *believe* with flexibility but act according to the traditions.

In all this it must be remembered that, as with the Reformers and the Orthodox, there is a spectrum of opinions among Conservative Jews. Some Conservatives are very similar to Reform Jews while others are virtually Orthodox (and there's a lot in between too). Conservative Judaism is the 'broad church' of the people of Israel.

During the early twentieth century Conservative Judaism was the dominant form of Jewish faith. Now that honour has fallen to Reform Judaism, as previously mentioned. Nevertheless, the great rabbinical training college of Conservative Judaism, The Jewish Theological Seminary in New York, remains massively influential throughout the United States and beyond.

Zionism: the way back to the holy land

A final movement within Israel needs to be discussed before drawing our study of Judaism to a close. The movement is called Zionism – from the name of the hill upon which

Jerusalem is built – and it is not so much a faction of particular Jews as an enthusiastic stream among Jews of many different kinds.

In the late 1800s an Austrian journalist named Theodor Herzl began to argue publicly that the Jews should be allowed to found their own state, a political and geographical entity they could govern themselves. The growing anti-Semitism of Germany and elsewhere made this all the more urgent. His idea of 'Israel' as a *state* was quite different from the Classical Jewish vision of Israel as a spiritual family awaiting the messianic kingdom. Nevertheless, Herzl's programme caught on.

In 1897 the World Zionist Organization was founded. The viewpoint of the organization was simple: the international community should find a region somewhere in the world to which Jews could emigrate and in which they could establish a self-governing state. The British offered an uninhabited portion (15,000 square kilometres, or 5,800 square miles) of Uganda for this purpose; Argentina was another possibility. After some discussion, however, Zionists insisted that only the holy land, Palestine, would do.

Anti-Jewish fever in Europe climaxed, of course, in the horrors of Nazi Germany – prison camps, torture and attempted extermination. Following the Second World War, as the world learned of the extent of the cruelties against Jews, the United Nations resolved that the surviving Jews of Europe (and elsewhere) should be allowed to move to Palestine, where a small number of Jews (about 100,000) already lived. A section of the holy land was determined, new boundaries were drawn, and in May 1948 the modern State of Israel was created. Zionism had triumphed. The Jews had returned home. The World Zionist Organization still exists to gain international support for the Jewish cause in the State of Israel.

Needless to say, while the international community acted out of a desire to bring justice to post-holocaust Jews, the effect of this 'home-coming' on the local Palestinian population of the period was devastating. The Arab-Israeli war of 1948–49 gained more land for the State of Israel and left more than half a million local Palestinians displaced. Our world still reaps the consequences of these events. One suspects that new sufferings as well as glories lie ahead for the ancient people of Israel.

Judaism in brief

Foundational Judaism (2000–500 BC): the fundamentals of the faith are developed.

• God promises Abraham that he will become a great nation and that he will be a blessing to all nations. Circumcision is introduced as the sign of this covenant.

• The Jews living in slavery in Egypt are redeemed by God in a mass exodus (1200s BC). The Passover festival is introduced to commemorate the event.

• The 'Torah' is given by God to Moses at Mt Sinai – Israel now has its way of life revealed, developing into the Tanak, or Bible of Judaism.

• God promises that King David's throne would be eternal – here are the foundations of the Jewish belief in the Messiah.

• The first temple is built in Jerusalem (900s BC) as a place for atonement and the praise of Israel's God.

• After a long period of disobedience, Israel is invaded by the Babylonians, who destroy the temple (586 BC). The second temple is built (512 BC)

Interim Judaisms (500 BC–AD 100): Jewish factions compete for prominence.

• Sadducees are the aristocrats and priests; Essenes are the apocalyptic holy men; Zealots are the patriots who fight the Romans, and the followers of Yeshua (or Christians) are deemed heretics of a false Messiah.

• The (second) Jerusalem temple is destroyed by the Romans (AD 70).

Classical Judaism (AD 100–1800): one form of Judaism emerges triumphant and sets the course for the bulk of Jewish history.

• The Pharisees rise to prominence (AD 100) and govern the Jews.

• The rabbinic teachings are collected and compiled in the Mishnah (AD 200). Reflection on the Mishnah and Tanak lead to the production of the Talmud and the Midrash (AD 400–800).

Modern Judaisms (1800): Classical Judaism splits in three.
• Reform Judaism: a movement of deep integration with the Gentile world
• Orthodox Judaism: a movement insisting on separation from the Gentile world
• Conservative Judaism: a movement seeking a path between these two extremes

Facts and figures on Judaism today
• Judaism is the sixth largest religion in the world with over 14 million believers.[1]
• Jews make up .2% of the world's population.[2]
• Judaism is found in 134 countries worldwide.[3]
• Jerusalem, with 422,000 Jews, is the fourth largest urban Jewish population behind New York (1.75m), Miami (530,000), and Los Angeles (490,000).
• Of the estimated world population of 14 million Jews, around one third live in Israel. There are 5.8 million Jews in the United States.
• Jews were highly involved in establishing the early Hollywood film studios including Twentieth Century Fox, MGM and Warner Brothers.

[1, 2, 3] *Britannica Book of the Year 2004*, Encyclopaedia Britannica Inc. (p 280)

Famous Jews
Woody Allen
Well-known film director whose films are almost all set in New York City. Frequently casts himself in the role of a neurotic New Yorker.

Sigmund Freud (1856–1939)
Developed the science of the mind called psychoanalysis.

Albert Einstein (1879–1955)
Most famous and influential scientist of the twentieth century and peace activist.

Good books and sites on Judaism today

http://www.torah.org

http://judaism.about.com

www.jewishencyclopedia.com

Neusner J., *The Way of the Torah: an introduction to Judaism*. Belmont (Ca.): Wadsworth Publishing, 1997.

Jacobs, L., *The Jewish Religion: a companion*. Oxford: Oxford University Press, 1995.

Grabbe, L. L., *An Introduction to First Century Judaism: Jewish Religion and History in the Second Temple Period*. Edinburgh: T & T Clark, 1996.

Smart, N. and Hecht, R. (editors), 'Judaism', in *Sacred Texts of the World: a universal anthology*. New York: Crossroad, 2002, 45–89.

Smart, N., *The World's Religions* (2nd edition). Cambridge: Cambridge University Press, 2003, 246–274.

Christianity
The Way of the Christ

In a nutshell

Christianity could be described as the belief and practice of those who revere Jesus Christ as the one who taught how people ought to live, died for the sins of the world and rose again so that people might live with God (and one another) forever.

17 Jesus and the sources of Christianity

The word 'Christianity' tells you a couple of very important things about the topic of the next few chapters. Firstly, it lets you know that the faith of Christians has a lot to do with a person, Jesus Christ. Just how much it revolves around this man will soon become clear.

The other thing the word 'Christianity' tells you is that this Faith is intimately related to ancient Judaism. The word 'Christ' is an important Jewish term. It is not a surname like 'Dickson' – Jesus' parents were not Mr and Mrs Christ. As I said in chapter 13, 'Christ' means 'Anointed One' and is the title given by Jews to the king God will one day send to redeem Israel and rule all nations. By naming Jesus the 'Christ' and his followers '*Christ*ians' (people of Christ), Christianity claims to fulfil the hopes of Judaism.

We begin by looking at the sources of our knowledge about Jesus.

Non-Christian sources about Jesus

Christianity arrived on the scene at a time of great literary activity: philosophers were writing weighty tomes on the meaning of life, poets and playwrights were composing material to make people laugh and cry, emperors were crafting royal propaganda to ensure they were remembered, and historians were recording for posterity all that they could discover about their cultural heritage. The non-biblical writings of the first few centuries AD would fill many shelves in a modern library.

One lucky outcome of this flurry of literary activity is that a Palestinian teacher, named Yeshua, or Jesus, managed to get a mention in several Roman, Greek and Jewish writings of the time. Some of the references are neutral; others are downright antagonistic, like my personal favourite from Cornelius Tacitus (AD 56–120), ancient Rome's most famous historian:

Christians derived their name from a man called Christ, who, during the reign of Emperor Tiberius had been executed by sentence of the procurator Pontius Pilate. The deadly superstition, thus checked for the moment, broke out afresh not only in Judaea, the first source of the evil, but also in the City of Rome, where all things hideous and shameful from every part of the world meet and become popular (Annals 44.2–5).

Other first-century writers who mention Jesus include the Greek historian Thallos, the Syrian writer Mara bar Serapion, and the Jewish aristocrat Flavius Josephus, who mentions Jesus on two occasions. In the second century a number of interesting, mainly critical, statements about Jesus are found in the writings of (1) the satirist and lecturer Lucian of Samosata, (2) the Greek intellectual Celsus, and (3) some of the rabbis of the Jewish Talmud (in *Baraita Sanhedrin* and *Baraita Shabbat*).

All in all, these non-Christian sources provide only the following sketchy details about Jesus' life:
- The name 'Jesus'
- The place and time-frame of Jesus' ministry
- The name of Jesus' mother, Mary
- The ambiguity of Jesus' conception/birth
- The name of one of Jesus' brothers, James
- Jesus' wide fame as a teacher
- Jesus' fame as a miracle worker/sorcerer
- The popular naming of Jesus as 'Messiah/Christ'
- The time of Jesus' execution – around the Jewish Passover festival (April)
- The manner of Jesus' execution (crucifixion)
- The Roman governor responsible for the execution, Pontius Pilate

- The involvement of the Jewish leadership in Jesus' death
- The coincidence of an eclipse at the time of Jesus' death
- The report of Jesus' appearances to his followers after his death
- The flourishing of a movement that began to worship Jesus after his death

Obviously, these non-Christian references provide little more than an outline of Jesus' life. Nothing can be gained from these sources, for instance, about what Jesus stood for, or what he wanted from his followers. For these details we have to turn to another set of documents from the first century – those written by his followers.

Christian sources about Jesus

It is generally acknowledged that our earliest and most reliable sources of information about Jesus come from those closest to the events. Hence, the Christian 'New Testament' (the counterpart to the 'Old Testament', or Jewish *Tanak*) takes centre stage in modern research into Jesus.

The most important of these New Testament documents, for understanding the mission and message of Jesus, are the so-called 'Gospels'. The word 'gospel' means 'grand news', and these semi-biographical accounts of Jesus' life claim to tell the grandest news of all. We possess just four Gospels composed in the first century:

1. *The Gospel of Mark* – probably written in the mid-60s AD by a man named Mark, a colleague of an original follower of Jesus called the apostle Peter. 'Apostle' means one sent out by Christ to proclaim the gospel.

2. *The Gospel of Luke* – probably written around AD 70 by Luke, a colleague of the apostle Paul who, like Peter, claimed to have seen Jesus (resurrected) after his death. Most historians believe Luke's Gospel includes lengthy quotations from at least three much earlier sources.

3. *The Gospel of Matthew* – probably written around AD 80 by followers of the apostle Matthew, another original follower of Jesus. Traditional Christians (and a few scholars) would prefer to say that Matthew himself penned this Gospel. Matthew's Gospel, like Luke's, appears to rely heavily on prior sources.

4. *The Gospel of John* – written sometime between AD 60 and 90 (there's lots of debate here) by one of two 'Johns'. Some argue it was written by the apostle John, a contemporary and eyewitness of Jesus. Others (the majority) think it was composed by another 'John' who was a disciple of the apostle John.

Another set of New Testament writings provides a further historical source for our knowledge about Jesus. The letters of Paul are a collection of correspondence from the apostle Paul to various Christian groups around the Mediterranean – in Corinth, Rome and elsewhere. These letters provide the *earliest* historical sources about Jesus, being written between AD 48 and 64. Passing references to Jesus in Paul's letters confirm that things like Jesus' descent from King David, his teaching about love, his 'Last Supper', his betrayal, death, resurrection and appearances were already widely known throughout the Mediterranean decades before the four Gospels were published.

In chapter 7 we noted that the Buddhist Scriptures were first written down 300–400 years after Siddhartha Gautama's death. In chapter 15 we discussed the Jewish Mishnah compiled 150 years after the death of many of the rabbis quoted in the work. As I also pointed out in those chapters, such time gaps do not make these writings unreliable records of the sacred material. In contrast to modern times, ancient men and women preserved the sayings of important teachers by using centuries-old techniques of memorization and verbal transmission. Only 10–20 per cent of people could read, so writing things down was actually not the most effective means of passing on a teacher's wisdom. 'Oral tradition', as this process was called, was the preferred method for many in antiquity.

What was true for Buddhists, Jews and (as we shall see) Muslims was equally true for the first Christians: oral tradition was regarded as the most trusted way to safeguard and pass on the sacred teachings. In the case of Christianity, this method was employed for a relatively brief period. The oral traditions about Jesus' life started to be written down within twenty years of the events themselves. We turn in the next chapter to explore some of these events in detail.

18 The life of Jesus of Nazareth

Jesus was born around 5 BC. I know that sounds odd: how could Jesus be born BC, *before* Christ? There is a simple explanation. The man who gave us the calendar distinction between BC and AD (*Anno Domini*, 'in the year of the Lord') was an Italian scholar of the sixth century named Dionysius Exiguus ('Denis the Little'). In proposing a new dating system, commencing with the birth of Jesus, Denis sifted through the available historical records to arrive at the most probable date for the first 'year of the Lord'. He missed by only a few years. Based on the historical information available today, however, modern scholars confidently place Jesus' birth between 6 and 4 BC.

Carpenter and king

Comparatively little is known of Jesus' childhood. All we can say with confidence is that he grew up in the district of Galilee (northern Palestine) in a little town called Nazareth where, like most Jewish boys, he would have followed in the trade of his father, Joseph. This meant Jesus was a carpenter, making and fixing furniture, fences and other household items. By our standards he was poor. By ancient norms he was about average.

More important than Jesus' trade was his ancestry. The Gospels of Matthew and Luke, as well as one of Paul's letters, indicate that Jesus was a descendant of King David (1000 BC), the greatest of Israel's kings and the one to whom God had promised an eternal throne (discussed in chapter 13). Not that having royal blood necessarily makes you special – my wife is a descendant of Robert the Bruce, first king of Scotland

(AD 1274–1329), and it comes with no perks whatsoever. However, as people began to suggest that Jesus was the promised Messiah, this connection with the ancient royal family became vitally important.

Preacher of the 'kingdom of God'

What Jesus did between his childhood and his adult career is completely unknown. That hasn't stopped some interesting speculation though. Recent New Age writers have surmised that Jesus journeyed to Egypt to learn magic, or to India to learn wisdom. Historical scholars offer more boring proposals. They figure Jesus probably did what most Jewish boys of the time did – stayed 'put' and worked with the family. If Jesus' father died early – as many historians suspect – the 'staying put' theory provides the only plausible scenario. Staying at home to look after his mother (Mary) and the other members of his extended family (six that we know about) would have been his moral duty until adulthood.

Sometime in AD 28, though, around thirty-three years of age, Jesus emerged from Galilee in the north of Palestine as a teacher. It is unlikely Jesus had any formal education, apart from what he got at home and in the local synagogue, and yet very quickly he seems to have attracted a great deal of attention.

People today often associate Jesus with words of simple spiritual wisdom: 'Turn the other cheek', 'Do unto others what you would have them do unto you', and so on. It is true that Jesus had a lot to say about ethics and relationships but most of this was not new. Much of his moral teaching was simply a reworking of traditions found already in the Jewish Torah.

The truly dramatic thing about Jesus' teaching was his daring announcement that the long-awaited 'kingdom of God' had arrived, or at least had come 'near':

Jesus went into Galilee, proclaiming the gospel of God. 'The time has come,' he said. 'The kingdom of God is near. Repent and believe the gospel!' (Mark 1:14–15).

It is difficult to convey just how explosive such a message would have been in first-century Palestine. Declaring that 'the kingdom of God is near' was equivalent to saying that everything the Jews longed for was finding fulfilment in their midst. It meant that the everlasting throne promised to King David (1000 BC) was being realized, that judgment upon evil was close at hand, and that all nations would finally submit to the one true God.

For Jews of this period the phrase 'kingdom of God' evoked strong political aspirations: the promised eternal throne was hoped to be an earthly throne, God's judgment upon evil was thought to be aimed at Rome in particular, and the submission of the nations to God was expected to involve the submission of the nations to Israel as well. Jesus' idea of the 'kingdom', however, was anything but political. Let me explain.

The 'friend of sinners'

At the heart of Jesus' message about the kingdom was the insistence that it was open to everyone – even to those normally thought to be excluded from God's plans and deserving of his judgment.

Ancient Judaism regarded 'lepers' (those with a range of skin diseases) as 'unclean', that is, in a state of impurity that excluded them from the life of Israel. Jesus touched lepers (reportedly healing them) and personally declared them to be 'clean', that is, approved members of God's family.

Another group of 'outsiders' was the tax collectors. Tax collectors were widely criticized by their fellow Jews as *traitors* for raising revenue on behalf of the Romans and *scoundrels* for getting rich in the process. Nevertheless, Jesus regularly sought out these 'greedy Roman lovers' and offered them God's mercy.

In first-century Palestine no one was considered more impure and deserving of God's judgment than a prostitute. And yet, on at least one occasion that we know of, while dining at the home of a Pharisee (see chapter 15 for details about the Pharisees), Jesus welcomed a prostitute to the table. The woman had heard Jesus was in town, and in her desperation to meet him she 'gate-crashed' the dinner party. Much to the displeasure of his religiously devout host, Jesus let this woman touch him as she wept at his feet hopeful of God's mercy. Jesus shocked everyone at the party by accusing his host of self-righteousness and offering divine forgiveness to the woman:

> *Then Jesus said to her, 'Your sins are forgiven.' The other guests begin to say among themselves, 'Who is this who even forgives sins?' Jesus said to the woman, 'Your faith has saved you; go in peace' (Luke 7:48–50).*

Perhaps not surprisingly, around this time, Jesus began to be slandered in public by conservative Jews as the 'friend of sinners', a tag Jesus may well have taken as a compliment.

It is a curious fact to remember that no person in the Bible spoke more about hell (the place of judgment) *and* about the forgiveness of sinners than did Jesus. He apparently viewed his mission as a *rescue* mission: an attempt to save people from a fate worse than death.

Forgiveness and the temple

Jesus' offer of forgiveness of sins was one of the most striking features of his ministry. On another occasion we are told that Jesus met a crippled man. Jesus reportedly healed him but also declared: 'My child, your sins are forgiven' (Mark 2:5). This was outrageous. 'Sins' are those things in human conduct that offend *God*, not Jesus. So how could Jesus go around forgiving sins? That was precisely the question the religious leaders wanted to ask: 'Why does this fellow speak in this way? It is blasphemy! Who can forgive sins but God alone?' (Mark 2:7).

As I explained in chapter 13, ancient Jews had highly developed rituals of forgiveness. These were conducted in the Jerusalem temple. The role of the priest in the process was merely to conduct the ceremonies and announce divine forgiveness to the worshippers. The priest did not actually forgive people's sins himself. That was God's business, according to Jewish theology.

Jesus seemingly cut right across this centuries-old tradition by claiming that if you were connected with him – were a member of the kingdom he talked about – you would be cleansed from all your sins. This was as good as claiming yourself to be a substitute temple, an alternative locus of God's presence and mercy.

Baffling deeds

The claim that Jesus performed unexplainable deeds is everywhere in our ancient sources – both Christian and non-Christian sources. Even the most critical specialists today, historians such as John Meier, John Dominic Crossan and Ed Sanders (to name just three from the sceptical end of scholarship) concede that, historically speaking, it looks as though Jesus performed deeds that everyone (including opponents) believed to be 'miraculous'.

The Gospels themselves cast Jesus not as a 'magician' – which is how the Jewish leadership of the day explained his abilities – but as the king of God's kingdom, the Messiah. It is in this context that we are to understand, what one non-Christian source described as, Jesus' 'baffling deeds' (*Jewish Antiquities* 18.63). According to the Gospels, Jesus possessed the very power of God to restore sight to the blind, hearing to the deaf, healing to lepers, strength to the paralyzed, and numerous other blessings to the sick and dying.

The widespread belief in Jesus' powers partly explains his great popularity throughout Palestine – a popularity that culminated in some very dramatic events.

Messiah comes to town

Toward the end of his three-year career as a preacher, healer and religious dissident, Jesus set his sights on Jerusalem, 100 kilometres (62 miles) south of his home district of Galilee. Jerusalem, of course, was the city King David had founded; it was the home of the ancient royal palace; and, most importantly, it was where the great temple stood.

When Jesus eventually went public, he didn't come out and declare, 'Friends, I am the long-awaited Son of David.' He chose to reveal his identity by acting out one of the most famous prophecies in the Old Testament (the Jewish *Tanak*) about the coming of God's king. In the book of Zechariah (written around 500 years before), the prophet predicted that the Messiah would arrive in Jerusalem riding on a 'donkey':

> *Rejoice greatly, O Daughter of Zion! Shout, Daughter of Jerusalem! See, your king comes to you, righteous and having salvation, gentle and riding on a donkey, on a colt, the foal of a donkey... He will proclaim peace to the nations. His rule will extend from sea to sea and from the River to the ends of the earth (Zechariah 9:9–10).*

According to the Gospels, Jesus arranged to enter Jerusalem in April AD 30 mounted – you guessed it – on a donkey. As he commenced his ride over the Mount of Olives and down into the ancient city, a crowd of pilgrims, aware of the significance of this act, began to shout in unison like fans at a football match:

> *Blessed is the one who comes in the name of the Lord! Blessed is the coming kingdom of our ancestor David! (Mark 11:9–10).*

And what did God's newly proclaimed king do once he entered the holy city? He went into the temple courts, a structure about the size of Sydney's Stadium Australia, and began to denounce the temple priests.

The temple courtyard at this time was filled with worshippers. It was the week leading up to the Passover festival, so Jews from all over the Roman world were making their pilgrimage to the holy city to take part in this most sacred day of the Jewish calendar. They were there, as discussed in chapter 13, to commemorate Israel's liberation from Egyptian slavery centuries before. A lamb would be sacrificed to recall the original Passover lamb whose blood was placed on the doorframes of Jewish homes. When God came in anger against the Egyptians that fateful night in the thirteenth century BC, he saw the blood of the lamb and preserved the Jewish families. His judgment fell upon Egypt but *passed over* the Jews.

When Jesus entered the temple courts all those years later the temple officials were conducting business as usual, part of which included selling sacrificial animals (lambs, doves, etc.) to the visiting pilgrims. A lot of money changed hands at Passover time, and not all of it was honest. Jesus was disgusted:

He began to drive out those who were selling and those who were buying in the temple, and he overturned the tables of the money changers and the seats of those who sold doves; and he would not allow anyone to carry anything through the temple (Mark 11:15).

Jesus had criticized the religious leaders before. But this was taking dissent to a whole new level. Clearing out the temple courts was a dramatic symbolic public attack on the heart of Israel's leadership. Within days of this defining moment, Jesus would be dead.

The Jewish Passover and the death of Jesus

Jesus managed to avoid arrest for most of the coming week. His days were spent speaking to large crowds of pilgrims in the temple courtyard, before slipping away at night to a friend's home a few kilometres east of Jerusalem.

The final night was different. It was the eve of the Passover and Jesus wanted to celebrate this special occasion with his colleagues in the holy city itself.

When Jesus sat down to celebrate the Passover meal of AD 30, things would have proceeded in much the same way as they had for the 1,200 years before – cooked lamb, traditional spices, wine, unleavened bread, prayers, songs, and so on. But Jesus added one highly unusual element that evening. He took the bread and wine in his hands and gave them an intriguing new meaning:

> *Jesus took a loaf of bread, and after blessing it he broke it, gave it to the disciples, and said, 'Take, eat; this is my body.' Then he took a cup, and after giving thanks he gave it to them, saying, 'Drink from it, all of you; for this is my blood of the covenant, which is poured out for many for the forgiveness of sins' (Matthew 26:26–28).*

Jesus took the traditional Passover themes of 'blood' and 'forgiveness' and related them to what is about to happen to him. Jesus' blood, just like that of the Passover lamb, would be poured out for the forgiveness of God's people. God's judgment would fall upon the 'lamb' (Jesus) so that it might *pass over* 'sinners'. This, according to Jesus, was his destiny. This was how the undeserving could be welcomed into his kingdom.

Within hours of this Last Supper, Jesus was arrested, put on trial and found guilty of 'blasphemy' and 'crimes against the temple'. However, at this time, Israel was an occupied territory. The Jewish leadership (mainly the priestly Sadducees) did not have the authority to administer the death penalty. That power lay with the Roman prefect of the region, Governor Pontius Pilate, who saw Jesus' claim to be Messiah as a treasonous challenge to the authority of the Roman emperor (Tiberius). In socio-political terms, it was the Romans who killed Jesus.

Political explanations of Jesus' death are just one way of looking at the event. Christians insist that the truest meaning of the event is found not in politics but in Jesus' own explanation of his death: '[T]his is my blood of the covenant, which is poured out for many for the forgiveness of sins.' According to the New Testament, Jesus died as a sacrifice for sins. He was the lamb for a worldwide 'Passover'.

The resurrection of Christ

If the Gospels had left Jesus in a martyr's tomb, this would have been a perfectly respectable way to conclude a story about a great Jewish teacher. Religious martyrs were widely revered in first-century Palestine. Contrary to all expectations, however, the first Christians insisted that the tomb in which Jesus was laid on Friday afternoon was empty on Sunday morning.

Explanations abound, of course: perhaps Jesus' followers stole the body and kept quiet about it to their deaths; maybe Jesus simply recovered from his injuries and convinced people he had been resurrected. Jesus' followers offered an entirely different explanation, and their claim launched a movement that would utterly transform the world: God, they said, had raised the Messiah from the dead.

The most significant statement about the resurrection, in the opinion of virtually all historians, is one tucked away in a letter of the apostle Paul to the new Christians in Corinth. The statement is important not simply because Paul claims in it to be an eyewitness but, more importantly, because the account of the resurrection cited here was probably crafted in the AD 30s – about as close to the events themselves as historians could hope for:

> For I handed on to you [Corinthians] as of first importance what I in turn had received [and here Paul quotes the account]: 'That Christ died for our sins in accordance with the scriptures, and that he was buried, and that he was raised on the third day in accordance with the scriptures, and that he appeared to Cephas, then to the twelve.' Then he appeared to more than five hundred brothers and sisters at one time, most of whom are still alive, though some have died. Then he appeared to James, then to all the apostles. Last of all, as to one untimely born, he appeared also to me (1 Corinthians 15:3–8).

There are at least six separate appearances of the resurrected Jesus mentioned here: (1) to Cephas (Aramaic for 'Peter'), (2) to the twelve apostles together, (3) to 500 believers at once, (4) to James (Jesus' blood relative), (5) to all of the apostles (that is, missionaries beyond the group of the twelve) and, last of all, (6) to the writer of the letter himself, the apostle Paul, who had been a persecutor of the Christians up to that moment.

There is another set of witnesses to the empty tomb which (for whatever reason) is not mentioned in this statement. It is one that almost certainly belonged to the earliest reports about the resurrection. According to all four Gospels, the first people to know about the empty tomb and the resurrection of Jesus were not the (male) apostles but a small group of named women, including Mary (Jesus' mother), Salome, Joanna and (another) Mary. For historians, it is intriguing that this detail is mentioned. Women were widely regarded in the first century as unreliable witnesses. And, yet, without any apparent embarrassment, the Gospel writers concede that the first witnesses to the bizarre events following Jesus' death were all women.

Two things are agreed upon by most specialists in the field. Firstly, Jesus' tomb was empty some time after his crucifixion. Secondly, Jesus' followers experienced (what they believed to be) 'appearances' of their risen Messiah. Does this mean that historians can 'prove' Jesus rose from the dead? Some believe so; I personally do not. How people account for these twin facts (the empty tomb and the appearances) will depend largely on what they feel is possible in this world. If they reject the existence of a Being able to influence the world (God), they will probably look for a natural explanation of the facts: Jesus recovered from his wounds, for example. If, on the other hand, one accepts the possibility of God's influence in the world, one may well accept the New Testament explanation. It is not my purpose in this book to engage in arguments for this conclusion.

19 From Christ to the New Testament

I have emphasized throughout these chapters that what we call 'Christianity' was essentially a Jewish phenomenon. Jesus was a Jew, all of his first followers were Jews, and many Christians continued to attend their Jewish synagogues (as well as church) right throughout the first and second centuries. Only when the Pharisaic rabbis published an official curse on the Christians (around AD 100; see chapter 14) did Classical Judaism and Christianity really begin to part company.

From Judaism to Christianity

One of the striking things about the first Christians is the way they tried to work out how the news about Jesus' life, death and resurrection (the 'gospel' message, as they called it) ought to be brought to Gentiles (non-Jews). After all, according to the ancient prophecies, the Messiah was meant to rule 'from sea to sea and from the River to the ends of the earth' (Zechariah 9:10). Israel's Messiah was meant to be for every nation. These early followers of Jesus had some radical thinking to do.

The big issue here was 'circumcision'. The rite of circumcision had long been regarded as the key sign of belonging to God's family Israel. So the question for the first Christians was: should Gentiles who want to follow Christ also be circumcised? Put another way, should Gentiles become fully fledged Jews in order to be real Christians? It may surprise you to know that many of the first Christians answered 'yes' to this question. This made 'conversion' to Christianity for male Greeks and Romans a very difficult process (if you know what I mean).

After vigorous debate between conservative Christians and more liberally minded ones, a decision was made (at a council in Jerusalem in AD 48) that would have huge significance for the religious landscape of the world. It was determined that although 'circumcision' was the sign of membership in Israel, it was not necessarily the sign that you followed Israel's *Messiah*. Gentiles could henceforth enjoy the benefits of Jesus' kingdom as Gentiles, without circumcision.

The first world religion

The effect of this decision cannot be overstated. Suddenly, this small Jewish movement exploded throughout the Roman world. Preachers, such as the apostles Peter and Paul (and hundreds of others), took this news to the farthest reaches of the empire. Wherever they went they established 'churches', small groups of believers who would gather together to pray, sing songs, learn more about Christ and eat meals in his honour. The word 'church' simply means *gathering*.

The message of the apostles was a 'hit'. By the early 50s AD churches were meeting in homes, halls and outdoor venues in some of the most thriving cities of the pagan world – Antioch in Syria, Ephesus in Turkey, Corinth in Greece and Rome in Italy. Within three centuries an estimated 30 million people would consider themselves Christian – that was half of the Roman world. Christianity was on its way to becoming history's first world religion. As Professors Ernst W. Benz and Martin E. Marty conclude in their *Encyclopaedia Britannica* entry on Christianity:

> *The missions and expansion of Christianity are among the most unusual of historical occurrences. Other world religions, such as Buddhism and Islam, also have raised a claim to universal validity, but no world religion other than Christianity has succeeded in realizing this claim through missionary expansion over the entire world.*

Letters to the churches

Many of the New Testament books – the books regarded by Christians as sacred – were simply letters sent by the first Christian leaders to the recently founded churches scattered throughout the Roman world. The book of 1 Corinthians, for example, is one of two letters in our possession written by the apostle Paul to a group of new Christians meeting in Corinth. Some New Testament books were 'circulars', that is, letters intended for distribution among a number of Christian communities. One such book is James, a letter sent by a relative of Jesus, named James, to Christian groups scattered throughout the Mediterranean.

These early Christian leaders were greatly revered because of their contact with Jesus. As a result, their writings were preserved. Copies of their letters were also made, and these were passed on to other churches so they too could hear what the apostles had to say on such wide-ranging issues as sex, money, marriage, politics and suffering, as well as subjects like God, death and the future.

Over time, hundreds of copies of these letters were circulating throughout the Roman empire, bringing a rich source of instruction and encouragement to the ever-growing Christian community. These letters, along with the four Gospels, make up what Christians call the New Testament.

Whose New Testament?

Because of the popularity of the first-century Christian literature (the Gospels and the letters), groups in the second and third centuries began to produce similar material and tried to pass them off as original apostolic writings. These include the Gospel of Thomas, the Acts of Paul, the Letter of Barnabas, and many others. Eventually, churches all around the Mediterranean met in a series of councils, climaxing in the councils of Rome (AD 382) and Carthage, North Africa (AD 397). One purpose of these meetings was to determine which documents should be regarded as sacred and authoritative and which should be deemed otherwise.

The policy of these councils was highly *conservative*. Basically, they decided to embrace as Scripture only those documents that had long been recognized throughout the churches as penned by the first generation of Christian leaders, that is, by those whom Jesus appointed (Peter, Paul, James, etc), or by their immediate colleagues (Mark, Luke, etc.). Thus, these councils *culled* rather than *included*, leaving us with just twenty-seven books of the New Testament (the Gospels and the letters). The other writings (Gospel of Thomas, etc.) were published in separate collections and are all readily available in English translations today. They are of great historical interest for nerds like me because they tell us what some later Christians taught. But they do not help us hear the 'voice' of the first-century witnesses to Christianity. That voice, insisted the early church, could reliably be found only in the Gospels and letters of the New Testament.

Many thousands of ancient copies of the New Testament still exist today and are on display (inside sealed cabinets) in some of the great libraries of the world – the British Library in London, the Chester Beatty Library in Dublin, the library of the University of Michigan in the United States, and so on. Modern translations of the New Testament are made from these ancient manuscripts.

20 Major teachings of Christianity

The first-century Gospels and letters make up the New Testament. The New Testament together with the Old Testament (the Jewish *Tanak*) make up what Christians call the 'Bible' (from the Greek word *biblos* meaning 'book'). It remains now to unpack some of the major teachings of the Bible, as believed by mainstream Christians throughout the centuries. Then, in the following chapter, we can look at the distinctive teachings of the various 'brands' of Christianity.

Trinity: one God in three persons

I said earlier that one of the most striking aspects of Jesus' ministry was his insistence that God's forgiveness could be received directly through him, without needing to go to God's official dwelling place, the Jewish temple in Jerusalem. In a first-century Jewish context this was as good as claiming yourself to be a substitute temple, an alternative locus of God's presence and mercy. The scandalous nature of this claim is seen in the response of the Jewish leaders: 'Why does this fellow speak in this way? It is blasphemy! Who can forgive sins but God alone?' (Mark 2:7).

It is not an easy thought to ponder, but Jesus implied to his contemporaries that he personified the presence of God on earth. The one true God of Jewish history had entered into first-century history in the person of the Messiah.

What Jesus implied, numerous New Testament writers make explicit: Jesus and God are in fact *one*. The man from Nazareth is not merely the Messiah of Israel; he is God in the flesh. The

Gospel of John makes this point by describing Jesus as God's very 'Word' made 'flesh':

In the beginning was the Word (the one who would become Jesus), and the Word was with God, and the Word was God… The Word became flesh (Jesus) and made his dwelling among us (John 1:1, 14).

Here we have the beginning of the Christian doctrine of the 'Trinity'. The word 'trinity' means something like *three-ness*. It was coined by Christians of the second and third centuries as a way of saying in a single word what the Bible teaches in many words.

According to the Bible, God has revealed himself as the Father, the Son (that's Jesus) and the Holy Spirit. Now, the Father and the Holy Spirit were already known to Jews through statements in their *Tanak* (Old Testament). But it was never clear there whether the Holy Spirit was a distinct 'person' within God, or just a divine force.

The New Testament 'clarifies' this issue, describing the Holy Spirit as a fully divine person and yet distinct from God the Father. The first Christians then added to this picture by affirming Jesus also as fully God and yet distinct from both the Father and the Holy Spirit. The thought is captured well in the passage I just quoted from the Gospel of John: 'the Word (Jesus) was *with* God, and the Word *was* God'.

Without embarrassment, or any hint of contradiction, the Bible teaches that God is three persons sharing one divine nature. This does not mean that God simply appears in three modes, as H_2O can appear as either liquid or steam or ice. Nor does it mean that God has three different *parts*, as a triangle has three sides. As difficult as it is to comprehend – and I still get a headache thinking about it for too long – the biblical doctrine of the Trinity, believed by Christians of all varieties, states that the one true God exists as three equal persons. I suspect the doctrine of the Trinity rivals the Buddhist doctrine of the Five Aggregates of Attachment (discussed in chapter 8) for the Most-Difficult-Religious-Concept award.

The 'kingdom come': Christianity and the future

I said earlier that a central theme in Jesus' own teaching was what he called the 'kingdom of God', that is, God's rule (his kingship, if you like) over all things. According to Jesus and the New Testament, God's kingdom is both *present* and *future*. It is present in the sense that God's appointed king, the Messiah, has arrived within history, offering his mercy and leadership to all who want them. It is future, however, in the sense that this kingdom will be witnessed fully only at the end of history. With this in mind, Jesus urged his disciples to make the hope for the coming kingdom a part of their regular prayers. In the Lord's Prayer (or 'Our Father'), he taught his followers to say:

> *Our Father in heaven, hallowed [holy] be your name,*
> *Your kingdom come, your will be done,*
> *On earth as it is in heaven (Luke 11:9–10).*

Christians throughout the centuries have emphasized several aspects of this future kingdom. Firstly, Christians believe in a so-called 'Second Coming' of Jesus. In many ways, Jesus' appearance in first-century Palestine was a foretaste of his ultimate appearance. There is great debate over the details of the Second Coming, but all Christians agree that at Jesus' return human history will culminate and the kingdom of God will be fully known.

Secondly, according to Christians, God's future kingdom will begin with a Day of Judgment when God will weigh the conduct of every man and woman. In the Bible, this theme is presented not simply as a scare tactic designed to make us more religious but as a kind of pledge that God sees the injustices of history and will one day console the downtrodden faithful by righting the wrongs of the world. Christians know themselves to be part of the wrongs of the world but believe Jesus' death provides the means of escaping the judgment they would otherwise deserve.

The third and, perhaps, strangest aspect of the 'kingdom come', as believed by Christians of the last two millennia, has to do with the universe itself. Christianity does not envisage a kingdom of disembodied spirits floating upon heavenly clouds wearing halos and listening to harp music. That is the 'heaven' of Hollywood. The future kingdom taught by Jesus, and hoped for by all mainstream Christians, is a place in which human beings are resurrected and the creation itself is renewed. What Christianity promises to the faithful is nothing less than a 'new creation'. This is partly why the resurrection of Jesus is so important to Christianity. Christ's rising to life is believed to be God's pledge within history that he will raise us (and the creation) at the end of history. And so Christians add to their regular prayers, 'Our Father in Heaven... your kingdom come'.

'Grace': salvation as a gift

This emphasis on the future shouldn't obscure the fact that Christianity claims also to be a faith of the present. One example of the present benefits of Christian faith is the New Testament theme of grace. The word 'grace' has almost fallen out of usage in modern English, except as a girl's name and perhaps as a way of describing the movement of a ballerina: 'she dances with such grace!'

In the New Testament, the word 'grace' refers to the *unmerited gift of God's pardon*. God's mercy can be experienced here and now not as a reward for religious and moral effort but as an act of God's favour, his *grace*.

Many biblical passages treat the theme of grace. The word itself appears over 150 times in the New Testament (more often, in fact, than the word 'love'). The impetus for this emphasis on grace came from Jesus himself, who freely handed out God's mercy and gave up his life for the sins of the world.

In the history of Christianity there have been great debates about how exactly one receives God's grace, but all are agreed on this central point: membership in God's family (and in the future kingdom) is granted to believers not as a 'reimbursement' for hard work but as a gift of God's grace.

The love ethic: how Christians are to live

All Christians agree that believers are to respond to this grace by treating others with the kindness God has shown to us. In other words, Christianity calls on those who follow Christ to live by an ethic of love.

Jesus' command to 'love your neighbour' was not new. Jesus derived this teaching from his Jewish *Tanak*, or Old Testament. What was unusual about Jesus' teaching was his definition of 'neighbour' to include everyone, even one's enemies:

> *You have heard [from the rabbis of the day] that it was said, 'Love your neighbor and hate your enemy'. But I tell you: Love your enemies and pray for those who persecute you (Matthew 5:43–44).*

It is no exaggeration to say that the success of Christianity in the centuries immediately after Christ can be attributed in large part to the seriousness with which Christians took Jesus' command to love others in the way God had loved them. Huge daily food rosters became commonplace in the early churches. Orphanages were opened, hospitals were established and visitation programmes were implemented in the Roman prisons.

It is commonly believed by historians that the Jews were the first in antiquity to implement a welfare system for the poor, abandoned and dispossessed. Christianity inherited this practice but made one significant change, inspired by Jesus' teaching: Christian welfare was open to believers and unbelievers alike. Anyone could come to the ancient church for assistance. And they came in their thousands, much to the consternation of Roman officials.

The impact of the Christian ethic of love was so great in the ancient world that the fourth-century pagan emperor Julian feared the Christians might take over the world through the 'stealth' of good deeds. He even wrote to his priests insisting that pagan temples set up a welfare system similar to that operating in the Christian churches. He offered government assistance to get it off the ground. In one letter written in AD 362 Julian wrote to the pagan high priest of Galatia (modern

Turkey) complaining about the continued expansion of Christianity, which he calls 'atheism' because of its denial of the traditional pagan gods:

> *Why do we not realise that it is the Christians' compassion toward strangers, their care of the graves of the dead and the pretended piety of their lives that have done most to increase this atheism...* *For it is disgraceful that, when no Jew ever has to beg [because of Jewish welfare], and the impious Galilaeans [= Christians] support not only their own poor but ours as well, all men see that our people lack aid from us* (Letters 22. Works of the Emperor Julian *vol.3. Loeb Classical Library 29*).

As it turned out, Christianity did take over the Roman empire, in large part through its ethic of love. Rodney Stark, professor of sociology and comparative religion at the University of Washington, writes:

> *Therefore, as I conclude this study, I find it necessary to confront what appears to me to be the ultimate factor in the rise of Christianity... Christianity taught that mercy is one of the primary virtues – that a merciful God requires humans to be merciful... This was revolutionary stuff. Indeed, it was the cultural basis for the revitalization of the Roman world groaning under a host of miseries...* (The Rise of Christianity, *Harper Collins, 1997, 209ff*).

Unfortunately, once 'in power', the Christian church ended up being party to some spectacular acts of hatred as well- collaboration in the European Crusades against the Muslims in the eleventh century, the awful treatment of heretics in the Inquisitions of the fifteenth and sixteenth centuries, the unforgivable silence at Hitler's treatment of the Jews in the twentieth century, to name a few.

These deeds can hardly be explained, let alone excused. The only consolation for embarrassed Christians today is the knowledge that such behaviour is the antithesis of that practised by Christians in the centuries immediately after

Christ, when Christianity experienced its greatest expansion. In that period – and at least in theory today-Christ's ethic of love permeated Christian communities.

I want to conclude this discussion of major Christian beliefs by talking about two of the 'rituals' that have been part of Christianity since the earliest times. Both derive from Jesus' Jewish heritage.

Baptism: a ritual of cleansing

The first ancient Christian ritual is called 'baptism', from the Greek word *to dip*. Historians are not entirely sure when baptism emerged, but it seems clear that Jews had been practising the rite for at least a century before Christ.

The central idea in baptism is 'cleansing'. In its ancient Jewish form, it had to do with purifying yourself after some spiritually polluting activity, such as contact with Gentiles (non-Jews).

The first Christians inherited this Jewish ritual but changed it in one significant way. Baptism for Christians was a one-off event. When someone decided to follow Christ, taking hold of the grace he offered, that person was considered cleansed from all sin. The new believer (and his or her children) therefore took a kind of 'spiritual bath' designed to symbolize the removal of guilt before God.

In the third century some Christians began to question the practice of baptizing children. That debate continues today, with some Protestant denominations (notably the Baptists) insisting that baptism should not be performed until a person fully understands the meaning of the ritual. Nevertheless, baptism remains a central rite for all brands of Christianity.

The Lord's Supper: a ritual of connection with Christ

Another ritual going back to Judaism via Jesus is variously known as the Eucharist, Communion, or Lord's Supper.

Whatever you call it, Christians of every variety have celebrated their connection with Christ in this special 'meal'.

The Lord's Supper goes back to Jesus' Last Supper, when he gathered with his disciples to celebrate the Passover. During the course of the evening Jesus took bread, broke it and said, 'Take and eat; this is my body.' Then he took a cup of wine and passed it to his colleagues saying, 'This is my blood of the covenant, which is poured out for many for the forgiveness of sins.' Jesus added the words, 'Do this in remembrance of me.'

How often the first Christians re-enacted this 'remembrance' meal is unclear – they may have done it every time they met (in church), or perhaps just once a year at Passover time. Whatever the case, this 'meal' has come to occupy an important place in the practice of Christians ever since. In this Lord's Supper, Christians remember Jesus, they connect with Jesus, and they even *feed* on him. As they take the bread in their mouths, they realize afresh that Jesus' body was broken for them on the cross. As they sip the wine, they taste, as it were, Jesus' blood given for their sake. And so Christians are nourished spiritually.

While all Christians highly value the Lord's Supper, there is some difference of opinion over the exact nature of the ritual. This, along with some other points of disagreement among the major 'brands' of Christianity, is discussed in the next chapter.

21 Three brands of Christianity

I've focused above on important aspects of Christian belief and practice common to all mainstream versions of Christianity. In a brief and non-technical way I want now to explore the three major 'brands' of Christianity that exist today – the Roman Catholic Church, the Protestant Church and the Orthodox Church.

The Roman Catholic Church

The term Roman Catholicism refers to a worldwide collection of churches that look to the bishop of Rome, known as the Pope, as the divinely appointed head of Christianity. 'Catholic' comes from the Greek word for *universal*. Hence, the Roman Catholic Church is the universal church that takes its lead from Rome.

Several features of faith and practice are particular to Roman Catholicism.

1. *The authority of the Pope.* Firstly, as just mentioned, Roman Catholics regard the bishop of Rome to be the true leader of the worldwide Christian movement. Theologically, this belief is based on Christ's words to the apostle Peter: 'And I tell you that you are Peter (*petros* means 'rock'), and on this rock I will build my church' (Matthew 16:18). Peter later settled in Rome where he was probably executed by Emperor Nero (mid-60s AD). The 'bishop' (meaning *overseer*) who succeeded Peter in Rome inherited Peter's status as the 'rock' of the universal church.

Most churches from around AD 100–300 were quite happy to regard the bishop of Rome, called the 'Pope' (from the Latin for *father*) as the figurehead of the rapidly growing Christian movement. But it was not until the fourth and fifth centuries that an official doctrine of the Pope's universal authority in all matters of faith and morality was stringently affirmed. Even then, it must be noted that churches in the eastern part of the Roman empire – Greece, Turkey, Syria, Palestine and Egypt – maintained a degree of independence from Rome. These churches preferred to think of the Pope as the 'elder brother' among church leaders rather than as the 'father' of the whole church. These Eastern churches would come to be known as the Orthodox Church – more about that in a moment.

2. *The mother of Jesus.* A second striking feature of Roman Catholicism is the veneration of Jesus' human mother, Mary. The New Testament portrays Mary as a woman blessed and favoured by God. On this basis, Christian leaders between AD 150 and 350 began to write about Mary in increasingly reverential ways. By the fourth and fifth centuries Mary came to be referred to as 'Mother of God', a title of immense prestige. Many Roman Catholics pray to Mary. They ask her to approach Jesus for them and secure his favour on their behalf. They are quick to point out, however, that the veneration given to Mary is never to be thought of as comparable to the *worship* given to God – the Father, Son and Holy Spirit.

3. *Jesus' substantial presence in the Lord's Supper.* A third crucial element in Roman Catholicism has to do with the ritual of the Lord's Supper. In Roman Catholic tradition, Jesus is not simply remembered in the meal, he is literally fed upon in the bread and the wine. Using a complex philosophical idea known as 'transubstantiation' (*change of substance*) Roman Catholicism insists that the bread in this ritual really becomes Jesus' sacrificial body and that the wine really becomes Jesus' sacrificial blood. Hence, for Roman Catholics, the Lord's Supper has a sacrificial dimension. The priest in the Communion service (called a Mass) re-enacts the offering of Christ on our behalf. He therefore secures God's grace for

those taking part in the meal. It is fair to say that the Mass is the centre of Roman Catholic Church life.

4. *A larger Old Testament.* Fourthly, the Old Testament used by the Roman Catholic Church is slightly larger than that used by the Protestant and Orthodox churches. The number of books in the Roman Catholic Old Testament was determined by an ancient Greek version of the Jewish *Tanak* (often called the Septuagint) which was widely used by the early church. This Greek version contained about half a dozen small documents not included in the Hebrew version of the *Tanak*. It was the Hebrew *Tanak*, not the Greek one, that became the authorized Scriptures of Judaism. The Protestant and Orthodox churches today follow the official Jewish list of (Old Testament) books, and call the 'additional' documents of the Roman Catholic Old Testament 'Apocrypha' (Greek for *hidden away*).

The Protestant Church

Protestantism, as the name suggests, was born as a *protest* movement against the perceived excesses and errors of the sixteenth-century Roman Catholic Church. Popes were seen to be living as virtual kings in not-so-virtual palaces. Church officials were often regarded as greedy and grossly immoral. Perhaps of most concern to these *protesters* was a practice known as 'indulgences'. The church taught that the faithful could avoid some of God's future punishments by making contributions (in the form of money or produce) to the ecclesiastical coffers.

In this context, numerous priests began to hold public debates and publish booklets about church abuses (the printing press had recently been invented). These priests called for reform, particularly in the matter of indulgences. The call was heard by thousands, first in Germany, then throughout Europe. The result was the so-called Protestant Reformation.

It must be remembered that, initially, all of the reformers were devout Roman Catholics. The movement for reform was internal to the church – no one was suggesting that a new church should be founded, only that the universal church should be transformed by God's truth. The most vocal man in the early Reformation was a German scholar and priest named Martin Luther. Luther demanded many changes to his beloved church, particularly to the doctrine of indulgences. If salvation was by grace, argued Luther, how could (financial) acts of service to the church atone for our sins before God? The question was potent and it spread like wildfire throughout Europe.

Eventually, the major reformers were excommunicated from the church (by papal order) and so was born what is now an independent tradition of the Christian faith known collectively as the Protestant faith. It is made up of numerous independent denominations including Anglicans (or Church of England), Baptists, Presbyterians, Assemblies of God, Brethren and many more.

Several features characterize all Protestant churches and, not surprisingly, most of these are deliberate rejections of Roman Catholic tradition.

1. *Authority in the Protestant Church.* Protestant churches have no equivalent of the Pope. Although various forms of hierarchy exist in all Protestant denominations – Anglicans have 'Archbishops', for instance – none of these structures is viewed as infallible in matters of faith and morality.

For Protestants, the only authority viewed as infallible is the Bible itself. Hence, in Protestant churches the 'sermon' – a talk usually based on a Bible passage – has a central place in the church service.

2. *Emphasis on salvation by grace.* Protestants strongly emphasize the doctrine of grace. While Roman Catholics, too, ultimately believe that salvation is God's unmerited gift to the faithful, Protestant churches underline this fact regularly and pointedly. They publish books about it, compose hymns about it, deliver sermons on it, and embed it in their 'liturgies' (forms of public worship).

Shortly after the Protestant Reformation the Roman Catholic Church itself reformed the practice of indulgences (1562), bringing it closer into line with the New Testament teaching on grace. Protestants, however, insist that further reforms are needed if the Roman Catholic Church is to reflect this doctrine correctly. The debate is complicated and will probably not be resolved any time soon.

3. *Jesus' spiritual presence in the Lord's Supper.* All Protestant churches reject *transubstantiation*, the idea that the bread and wine of the Lord's Supper ritual actually become the body and blood of Jesus. Protestants emphasize the words of Jesus, 'Do this in *remembrance* of me', and insist that the meal is memorial rather than substantial. The person conducting the Communion service (an Anglican priest, a Baptist pastor, an Assemblies of God layperson, or whoever) does not re-enact Christ's sacrifice, or re-present Jesus to God. He or she merely leads the congregation in 'feeding' on Christ in a *spiritual* way.

The Orthodox Church

Unlike Protestantism, the Orthodox Church did not break away from (or was not excommunicated from) the Roman Catholic Church. In fact, one of the most important features of the Orthodox point of view is the belief that they stand in unbroken connection with the original apostles themselves. The word 'orthodox' means *of correct opinion*, and the churches of the Orthodox tradition literally view themselves as the preservers of the most pure and ancient form of Christianity.

I said earlier that the bishop of Rome (the Pope) was widely regarded in the early church as the figurehead of the rapidly expanding Christian movement. This was based on the Roman church's connection with the apostle Peter. Churches in the East, however (in Greece, Turkey, Egypt and elsewhere), did not believe the Pope's special status included infallible authority in matters of doctrine and morality. They too had once had apostles in their midst (the apostle John had resided in Ephesus in Turkey).

Disputes between these two geographical giants of Christendom continued. In the fourth century, the churches of the East and West disagreed over the appropriate date for Easter, the most important Christian festival (celebrating Christ's death and resurrection). Over the next few centuries, they disputed over the use of religious icons in worship (frowned upon in the West), the marriage of priests (forbidden in the West), and a complex theological point about the Holy Spirit. This final dispute triggered what is often called the Great Schism, or separation, between Western and Eastern Christianity (AD 1054). The church of the West would be known as Roman Catholicism. The church of the East would be called Eastern Orthodoxy, made up of the Greek Orthodox, the Coptic (Egyptian Orthodox), Russian Orthodox, Armenian Orthodox, and so on.

So, what is distinctive about Eastern Orthodoxy?

1. *Authority in the Orthodox Church.* Firstly, the Orthodox Church is governed not by a central pope but by individual bishops who have authority over their particular region or 'diocese'. The bishops of the various dioceses come together in councils, called 'synods', and collectively these form the true 'government' of the Orthodox Church. The Archbishop of Constantinople (modern Istanbul, Turkey) is regarded as the honorary head of worldwide Orthodoxy and is called the Ecumenical Patriarch.

2. *Salvation as sharing in the nature of God.* A second feature of the Orthodox Church is its emphasis on 'deification', or the believer's sharing in the nature of God.

One New Testament passage declares that God 'has given us his very great and precious promises, so that through them you may *participate in the divine nature*' (2 Peter 1:3). Philosophical reflection on this idea has led to the special Orthodox view of human salvation. Orthodox churches, like Roman Catholic and Protestant churches, believe of course that Christ died and rose again for our sins. However, particular emphasis is also given to the 'incarnation' – God becoming a man in Jesus. God became a human being, says the Orthodox Church, so that human beings might 'participate in the divine nature'.

When the Orthodox talk about 'deification' (sharing in the divine nature) they are referring to the restoration of human nature back to its original, God-filled character. According to Orthodox theology, when Adam and Eve disobeyed God, they lost their true nature as people 'made in the image of God'. From that time on, men and women were less than truly human, less than what the Creator had intended them to be. This situation was reversed when God himself took on human nature – in Jesus Christ – and so renewed humanity's share in the original divine nature. All who now participate in the ministry of the church 'participate in the divine nature' made possible by Jesus.

3. *The use of images in worship.* The third aspect of Orthodox faith I want to mention is the use of icons, or images, in the worship of God. As I just mentioned, Orthodox Christians place special emphasis on the incarnation (God becoming man). Icons are an extension of this idea. God revealed himself in the visible, tangible person of Jesus Christ. Religious paintings (of Christ, or Mary, or the apostles, and so on) continue this visible mode of engaging with God. The Orthodox will be quick to explain that they do not worship the images. They merely use them as 'windows' to the reality of God.

Christianity in brief

The life of Jesus of Nazareth
• Born around 5 BC and raised as a carpenter in Galilee
• Emerges in AD 28 as a famed healer, 'friend of sinners' and preacher of God's kingdom
• Executed during the Passover festival of AD 30 for his claim to be the Messiah
• Disciples discover an empty tomb and witness Jesus raised from the dead

From Christ to Christianity
• The followers of Jesus abandon circumcision as the sign for Gentiles of belonging to Christ
• As the gospel is proclaimed far and wide churches spring up throughout the Roman empire
• Christian leaders compose the letters (to churches) and the Gospels (about Jesus) that would form the New Testament

Major teachings of Christianity
• Trinity: the Father, Son and Holy Spirit share in one divine nature
• The 'kingdom come': when Jesus returns people will be resurrected and judged, and the creation will be renewed
• Grace: God's unmerited gift of salvation
• The love ethic: Christian life is to be characterized by love of all people, including one's enemies
• Baptism: a spiritual 'bath' celebrating God's forgiveness of sins
• The Lord's Supper: a 'meal' of bread and wine embodying Christ's body and blood given on the cross

Three brands of Christianity
• Roman Catholic Church: the worldwide church that looks to the Pope, or bishop of Rome, for final authority in matters of doctrine and morality.
• Protestant Church: the worldwide church that sought to reform perceived abuses in the sixteenth-century church and so split with Roman Catholicism.

• Orthodox Church: the worldwide church that originated in the eastern Roman empire and emphasizes salvation as sharing in God's own nature.

Facts and figures on Christianity today
• Christianity is the largest religion in the world today with over two billion followers.[1]
• Christians make up almost 33% of the world's population.[2]
• Christianity is found in 238 countries.[3]
• There are over currently over one billion Roman Catholics who comprise 17.4% of the world's population.[4]
• Over 100 million people say they are Christian but are not affiliated with any church.[5]
• There are currently over 440 million Protestants.[6]

[1, 2, 3, 4, 5, 6] *Britannica Book of the Year 2004*, Encyclopaedia Britannica Inc. (p 280)

Famous Christians include:
William Wilberforce (1759–1833)
British politician who led the fight to end slavery in British colonies.

J. R. R. Tolkien (1892–1973)
Author of *The Hobbit* and *The Lord of the Rings*

Rev. Martin Luther King Jr (1929–68)
Leader of the movement to gain civil rights for African Americans in the 1950s and 1960s.

Mother Teresa
The 'Saint of the Gutters', Mother Teresa founded an order of nuns called the Missionaries of Charity in Calcutta, India dedicated to serving the poor. She worked for around fifty years serving the poorest of the poor in Calcutta. She was awarded the Nobel Peace Prize in 1979.

Peter Garrett
Former lead singer of Australian rock group Midnight Oil, now a politician with the Australian Labor Party.

Mel Gibson
Movie star and director of *The Passion of Christ*.

Good books and sites on Christianity
http://www.christianitytoday.com (leading Protestant website)

http://www.vatican.va/phome_en.htm (official English language website of the Roman Catholic Church)

http://www.oca.org (official site of the Orthodox Church in America with links to the worldwide Orthodox Church and its beliefs)

McGrath, A. E., *An Introduction to Christianity*. Oxford: Blackwell, 1997.

Frend, W. H. C., *The Early Church: from the beginnings to 461*. London: SCM Press, 2003, 1966.

Bockmuehl, M., *The Cambridge Companion to Jesus*. Cambridge: Cambridge University Press, 2001.

Dickson, J. *Simply Christianity: beyond religion*. Sydney: Matthias Media, 1999.

Johnson, P., *A History of Christianity*. New York: Touchstone Books, 1976.

Stark, R., *The Rise of Christianity*. New York: HarperCollins, 1997.

Smart, N. and Hecht, R. (editors), 'Christianity', in *Sacred Texts of the World: a universal anthology*. New York: Crossroad, 2002, 91–124.

Smart, N., *The World's Religions* (2nd edition). Cambridge: Cambridge University Press, 2003, 246–284, 326–347.

Islam
The Way of
Submission

In a nutshell

**Islam, from the Arabic word for submission, is a life
of surrender to the ethical and ceremonial will of
Allah (God) as revealed in the Koran and modelled in
the life of the Prophet Muhammad.**

22 Getting beyond September 11

Since September 11 2001 talking about Islam is a whole lot trickier. Non-Muslims in the West seem to divide into two passionate camps. On the one side are those who criticize Islam as a violent religion, a force bent on blowing up buildings, mistreating women and ruining the 'Western' way of life. One wonders how many people in this camp have actually met a Muslim or bothered to find out about the Islamic faith.

Another group respond with equal enthusiasm. Rightly worried about the first approach, some Westerners took it upon themselves to defend Islam. They insist that Muslims are peace-loving, 'just like us'. 'Fundamentalist Muslims', they say, are not real Muslims. They are a fraudulent minority with about as much connection to Islam as the Klu Klux Clan has to Christianity. For people in this camp, any discussion of Islam that did not present it as a model of compassion and democracy was labelled 'bigoted' and 'naïve'.

My own response to September 11, for what it's worth, is more in line with the sentiments of this second group. I suspect though that many of my fellow 'defenders' of Islam know as little about the religion as those who criticize it – though their motives are certainly kinder. The result among the 'defenders' is a weird 'Westernization' of Islam. We somehow transformed it in our minds into an ideal expression of Western values. The logic was simple: we are good; Islam is good; so Islam must be just like us. Few of us stopped to wonder if Islam might be 'good' without being anything like us.

Throughout these chapters it is important that readers try to put aside their assumptions about Islam – whether you are a 'critic' or a 'defender'. Basically, we have to try not to let the shadow of September 11 obscure our view of Islam. For example, mention is made in what follows about some early Islamic wars. I ask readers not to take this as proof that Muslims advocate violence, nor to take it as evidence that I have some lurking desire to cast Islam in a negative light. The fact of the matter is that war was a feature of early Islamic history. It would be virtually impossible to narrate the birth of Islam without referring to its early military successes. This, however, does not mean that violence is a necessary feature of Islamic faith.

We begin by looking at the life of the 'founder' of Islam, Muhammad.

23 From merchant to messenger of God: the life of Muhammad

When we discussed the life of Siddhartha Gautama (the Buddha) we saw that the accounts of his life were written centuries after his death. Even so, most historians believe that it is possible to reconstruct a broadly reliable account of the great man's life. Ancient people, as I've said before, were much better than we are at memorizing and passing on narratives: I have problems retelling jokes. This point is worth remembering as we turn to ask: *How* and *what* do we know about Muhammad?

The sources about Muhammad's life: Sira and Hadiths

Our best knowledge of Muhammad's life comes from two sources. The first is a biography of Muhammad's life written about 125 years after his death by a Muslim scholar named Ibn Ishaq (AD 704–767). The biography is called the *Sira* ('life'), and after some further revision in the early ninth century AD it came to be regarded as the official account of Muhammad's life. It ranks as one of the truly important books of the Islamic faith.

The second source of our knowledge of Muhammad is the *Hadiths* ('reports'). The *Hadiths* are a vast collection of individual reports about the words and deeds of Muhammad collected two to three centuries after his death. They are the accounts remembered and passed on by his early disciples. Many statements in the *Hadiths* begin with a reference to this passing-on of a report from one authority to another. Take this *hadith*, for example, which passes on a quotation of Muhammad about fasting:

> *Muhammad b. Rafi (not the Prophet Muhammad himself) has related to me, on the authority of Abd al-Razzaq, on the authority of Ibn Jurayj, from Ata, from Abu Salih al-Zayyat, that he heard Abu Hurayra say: the Apostle of Allah (i.e., Muhammad) said, "Allah – mighty and majestic is He – has declared: 'Every good work a man does is done for himself save fasting, which is done for Me, wherefore I Myself shall reward him for it'"* (Sahih Bukhari *Volume 7, Book 72, Number 811).*

Because of their relatively late date there is debate among Western historians about the reliability of the *Sira* and *Hadiths*. The kinds of questions raised about the first Buddhist, Jewish and Christian documents also surface in connection with the *Sira* and *Hadiths*. Muslims are probably right, however, to point out that the practice of passing on oral tradition had a long history in Middle Eastern societies. As I have emphasized, before the invention of the printing press (in the fifteenth century), this was the principal way cultures preserved their heritage.

I don't want to ignore the insights of modern historians, but it is important in a book like this to offer readers an account of Muhammad's life that reflects the Muslim perspective, not the watered-down scholarly one. Hence, in what follows I have tried to reflect a *traditional* Islamic account of the life of their founder.

From orphan to Prophet

Muhammad ibn Abdullah (the son of Abd Allah) was born in AD 570 (or perhaps 571) in the bustling commercial city of Mecca in central western Arabia. Mecca was not only a centre of trade, it was also a focus for religious beliefs from all over pagan Arabia. At the heart of the city was a huge box-like building called the *Kaba*. In it were housed the 360 idol-gods of Arabia. Prior to Islam, Arabia was mainly 'polytheistic' (many gods) in outlook – except, of course, among the Jewish and Christian communities scattered throughout the region. This *Kaba* building would become an important symbol in the story of Islam; it is still there today in the centre of the Great Mosque of Mecca (more about that later).

Getting back to Muhammad himself, tragedy struck early on. Before he was born his father died. Then, when he was only six, his mother died too. After a brief period with his grandfather, who died when Muhammad was eight, he was cared for by his uncle, Abu Talib, who was a prominent clan leader in Mecca and a successful international trader. Muhammad's early life was filled with a rich variety of cultural and business experience.

As he grew, Muhammad displayed a flair for trading. Indeed, while managing the goods of a wealthy Meccan widow named Khadija, Muhammad so impressed the woman that she offered herself to him in marriage. Khadija and Muhammad were married in AD 595. Muhammad was twenty-five; his bride was forty. Khadija was the first of eleven wives for Muhammad, which was not unusual at the time. She bore him three sons, who died in infancy, and four daughters.

Muhammad was a contemplative man, and he loved to leave the hustle and bustle of the city to go up into the mountains surrounding Mecca to a solitary cave where he could ponder the mysteries of life. Then one day in AD 610, during the Arabic month of Ramadan, something unexpected happened, something that would change Muhammad's life – and the course of history – forever.

According to Muslim tradition, the forty-year-old businessman from Mecca heard a heavenly voice repeating the word, 'recite'. Muhammad didn't know what to 'recite' until finally the voice – identified as that of the angel Gabriel – explained to Muhammad that he had been chosen as a 'Messenger of God' to restore to the world the truth about the Creator. The relevant *hadith* (report) states:

Ibn Humayd has related to me on the authority of Salma, from Muhammad b. Ishaq… Said the Apostle of Allah (Muhammad) – upon whom be Allah's blessing and peace: 'He (Gabriel) came to me while I was asleep, bringing a silken cloth on which was some writing. He said: "Recite; but I answered: What shall I recite?" Then he so grievously treated me that I thought I should die, but he pushed me off and said: "Recite." I answered: "But what shall I recite?"… He said: "Recite, in the name of your Lord who created – created man from clots of blood. Recite! Your Lord is the Most Bountiful One, who by the pen taught man what he did not know." So I recited it, and that ended the matter, for he departed from me. Thereupon I awoke from my sleep and it was as though he had written it on my heart' (Sahih Muslim Book 1, Chapter 74).

From that moment on, Muhammad was referred to by his followers as the 'Prophet'. In the remainder of the book I will follow this conventional way of referring to the founder of Islam.

Over the next twenty-two years (until his death in AD 632) the Prophet received frequent revelations of this type. After each encounter he would commit the messages to memory (or writing). These messages were proclaimed to all who would listen and then eventually compiled in a book that would become the central holy book of Islam, the Koran (also spelt Quran), meaning 'Recitation'.

For Muslims the Koran is not a product of Muhammad's creative ability – some of the traditions say he was illiterate. It is rather the record of the actual words of God. When I was given my first Koran by a Muslim leader in Sydney some years ago he asked me to be careful never to put the book on the ground and always to wash my hands before handling it. The reverence shown by Muslims to this Word of God is difficult to overstate.

According to the *Sira* and the *Hadiths* Muhammad was reluctant at first to accept his role as God's Messenger. He thought he might be going insane, or else was being tricked by some evil spirit. However, after the encouragement of his wife and his wife's cousin (who was a Christian) Muhammad eventually embraced this new responsibility and began to promote his revelations throughout his home city of Mecca.

These reluctant beginnings stand in stark contrast with the zeal that would soon envelop Muhammad as he began to gather together a small band of committed followers. Among his first converts in Mecca was his son-in-law, Ali. Remember that name because Ali would become a towering figure in Islam. He was the fourth leader (*caliph*) of the Muslim community after the death of the Prophet, and for millions of Muslims today (the *Shi'ites*) he is an object of deep devotion. But more about that later.

Rejection in Mecca

How did the people of Mecca react to this one-time businessman turned Prophet of God? Not very well, actually. At least, not in the early days.

We will look at the content of Muhammad's revelations later. For now, I just want to mention two aspects of his message that greatly threatened the governing officials of Mecca. The first was his insistence that there is just *one* God, Allah. The word 'Allah' had been used by Meccans for centuries to describe the supreme god who governed the other divinities (all 360 of them). Muhammad, however, insisted that Allah was not simply the head-god, he was the sole God. All the idols of the Meccan *Kaba* (that big, box-shaped building) were simply illusions, said the Prophet; they were false gods. This was like telling the curators of the Louvre in Paris that all of their works of art were fakes.

Muhammad gave the leaders of Mecca another cause for concern: he said that on Judgment Day Allah would overthrow anyone who mistreated the poor. Reminiscent of Jesus, and of the Old Testament prophets before that, Muhammad proclaimed a message of justice for all. Given that Mecca was a centre of commerce and trade you can imagine that ideas such as equity and charity were not terribly popular.

Naturally, all of this didn't go down well with the power-brokers of Mecca, and tensions began to boil over. For close to a decade Meccans resisted Muhammad's preaching as a minor annoyance. Toward the end of that time, however, things got tense and potentially dangerous. Muhammad decided (or was forced) to 'emigrate' to a city north of Mecca called Medina. A new phase of the Prophet's life was about to begin.

Acceptance in Medina: the first Muslim state

Medina was a nice safe distance from Mecca (over 400 kilometres, or 250 miles) and the people of the city were far more receptive of Muhammad's message. This signalled a turning point, and in many ways marked the real beginning of the religion we call Islam.

At Medina the Prophet was able to establish a community centred on two things: belief in Allah as the one true God, and commitment to Muhammad as Allah's messenger. But Muhammad was far more than the guru-figure of this new religious community. At Medina he was elevated to the position of a civil ruler. And so was born the first Islamic state (the *umma*), a very important concept for Muslims.

So important was this turnaround in the Prophet's career that the year AD 622 (the date of the founding of this first Islamic state) marks the beginning of the Muslim calendar. In the Islamic world the year of the first publication of this book is not AD 2004 but AH 1424. 'AH' stands for the Latin *anno Hegirae*, 'in the year of the emigration' to Medina. In other words, as I am writing this book it is 1,424 years after Muhammad moved from Mecca to Medina to create the first Islamic state.

For the mathematically minded, you may have noticed that 622 (the year of Muhammad's move to Medina) plus 1424 does not add up to 2004. It actually makes 2046. This is because the Muslim year is the shorter lunar year, based on the twelve cycles of the moon. There are about 354 days in a lunar year. The Muslim year goes more quickly than the Western (more correctly, 'Julian Calendar') year.

Life in Medina was not trouble free. To begin with, not everyone in the city was happy to accept Muhammad's status as the Prophet. There was a sizeable Jewish community in the city at the time. Although Jews approved of Muhammad's 'monotheism' (belief in one god), they remained sceptical about his claim to speak on God's behalf. Jews, of course, had their own prophets in the Torah.

The initial solution to this problem involved a simple treaty with the Jewish communities. Muhammad would recognize the Jews as a legitimate independent community as long as they remained politically loyal to the Muslim majority. Stability in the first Islamic state was ensured for the moment.

The quest for Mecca

Not so stable were relations with those in the city of the Prophet's birth. Many Meccans regarded Muhammad as a traitor and a threat to Arabian life. This impression was not helped by a series of raids conducted by Muhammad against Meccan trade convoys, or 'caravans'. It might be difficult for a Western reader at this point to envisage a founder of a religion engaging in battles. You should remember though that Muhammad was not simply a *prophetic* figure; he was also very much a political leader and a successful military commander. In seventh-century Arabia there was no separation between religion and politics.

Tensions between the Muslims of Medina and the 'pagans' down south in Mecca reached a high point in AD 624. Pagan Meccan forces came to a town near Medina called Badr. Muhammad's men were massively outnumbered – about three to one. Despite the odds, Muhammad and his Muslim fighters gained a fantastic victory over the unbelievers. This 'Battle of Badr' is regarded by Muslims as a sign of the supremacy of Allah over the false gods of the world. The Koran refers to this battle in the following way:

> It was not you, but God, who slew them. It was not you who smote them: God smote them so that He might richly reward the faithful (Sura 8:17).

Many other skirmishes took place during these years and in one of them (in AD 625) Muhammad himself was injured. Slowly but surely, however, the forces of the Prophet grew in number and prestige; so much so that the mighty city of Mecca was forced (in AD 628) to sign a truce with Muhammad. This allowed Muslims in Medina to make pilgrimages down to Mecca to visit the birthplace of the Prophet.

In AD 629 Muhammad accused the Meccans of breaking the terms of the agreement. He marched on the city with 10,000 men. Mecca was powerless. The citizens readily converted to Islam and Muhammad gladly accepted them. He preferred to offer amnesty than to wield a sword against the people of his birthplace.

Jihad: striving for Allah

A comment is probably needed at this point about the much discussed concept of *jihad*, often wrongly translated 'holy war'. The word *jihad* means simply 'struggle' or 'striving' and in its broadest sense refers to any *struggle* to be a good Muslim.

In some texts of the Koran the word *jihad* does refer to a military 'struggle'. Consider this passage:

Fight (jihad) for the sake of God those that fight against you, but do not attack them first. God does not love aggressors. Slay them wherever you find them. Drive them out of the places from which they drove you. Idolatry is more grievous than bloodshed. But do not fight them without the precincts of the Holy Mosque unless they attack you there; if they attack you put them to the sword. Thus shall the unbelievers be rewarded: but if they mend their ways, know that God is forgiving and merciful. Fight against them until idolatry is no more and God's religion reigns supreme. But if they desist, fight none except the evil-doers (Sura 2:190–193).

In a seventh-century Arabian setting, armed struggle like this was a normal part of life. Muhammad was no more warrior-like than any other clan leader of his time; in many ways, he was much more just and compassionate. The passage I just quoted is an important one because it makes clear in the opening lines that *jihad* is not to involve a pre-emptive strike: 'do not attack them first'. Many Muslims today stress that the 'Islamic terrorism' we see in various parts of the world contradicts this clear teaching of the Koran.

Muhammad was a revered soldier and commander, and the practice of military *jihad* over the following years and centuries contributed significantly to the new religion's success throughout the Middle East and beyond. This is not to say that Islam 'beat' the world into submission to Allah; far from it. Muhammad (and later Muslim commanders) customarily gave communities three options when they came into contact with Islamic expansion:

1. *Conversion.* Firstly, communities could convert to Islam and become part of the great Muslim community, or *umma*. This brought great privileges as well as responsibilities, and many towns and villages gladly embraced this course.

2. *Protection.* Secondly, communities could seek the status of 'protected peoples' (*dhimmis*). This meant that a community could keep its way of life (under the protection of the Prophet) but was obliged to pay a tax to the wider Muslim community. The Jews of Medina lived under this agreement until they were accused of treachery and were crushed (women and children were spared).

3. *Battle.* The third option available to non-Muslim peoples in the regions of Islamic growth was to take their chances in battle against the might of the Muslim sword: no small task! Only when a community refused to accept option (1) or (2) would Muhammad be forced to wield the sword in military *jihad*.

Muhammad was not blood-thirsty, and several texts in the Koran urge moderation in warfare. Muhammad was simply convinced that Islam had to spread throughout the world as a cleansing force. Within a decade Islam had won the allegiance of most of the people of Arabia, Persia and Egypt. Soon after the Prophet's death, Islam would spread to Palestine, Morocco and even Spain.

In thinking about *jihad* it is important to realize that modern Muslims, aware of the original meaning of the term in several texts of the Koran, choose to interpret this concept in spiritual not military terms. For a large proportion of the Muslims you are likely to meet in the Western world *jihad* is simply the 'struggle' to remain pure in an impure world. It is the 'fight' against sin and the devil and has nothing to do with taking up arms in the service of Allah. This point needs to be stressed again and again in our modern context.

The death of Muhammad and the leadership of Islam

By around AD 630, (twenty years after his call to be Prophet) Muhammad was the undisputed leader of all Arabia. He was the commander of the army, the head of state and the infallible spokesman for Allah. Two years later, at the age of sixty-two, the Prophet made his final pilgrimage to Mecca. When there he delivered a farewell sermon to his Meccan followers. In this address he urged them to remain faithful to Allah and loyal to one another as brothers (and sisters) in the worldwide *umma* (Islamic community). Returning to Medina, Muhammad fell ill and died in June AD 632. An extraordinary life had come to an end.

After the death of the Prophet the leadership of Islam fell to Abu Bakr, Muhammad's most trusted advisor and one of his fathers-in-law. Abu Bakr's title was *caliph*, which means 'deputy' (as in 'deputy' of the Prophet). The term is still used by *some* Muslims to refer to their preferred leader of the Islamic world. Abu Bakr was not regarded as a 'prophet'. His authority was mainly legal and military. This first *caliph* initiated several great conquests in the further expansion of Islam, notably over Iraq, Syria and Palestine.

In the decades following Muhammad's death a growing tension arose over how to determine the rightful leader of Islam. No one could replace the Prophet – everyone agreed on that-but the question remained: Who is the appropriate ruler of the Islamic community? Disagreement over this question would eventually split Islam in two.

24 Types of Islam

Tension in the air

To understand the differences between the major 'parties' of Islam we have to go back to the year of Muhammad's death in AD 632.

When the Prophet died there was, as I said, a crisis over who should lead the growing Islamic community (the *umma*). Muhammad does not appear to have explicitly appointed anyone to take his place.

The first three leaders of Islam, called *caliphs*, were all close companions of the Prophet:

Caliph 1. Abu Bakr was an advisor to Muhammad and the father of one of Muhammad's wives. He led for three years (AD 632–634).

Caliph 2. Next was Umar, who enjoyed a reputation as one of the greatest military leaders of his era. He led for a decade (AD 634–644). Shortly before he died, Umar appointed a selection committee to elect the next *caliph* once he was gone.

Caliph 3. The selection committee chose a leading man of Mecca named Uthman. He led for about twelve years (AD 644–656). So far so good.

Things appeared to be going well until the fourth *caliph* was chosen, a man named Ali. Ali was Muhammad's son-in-law, the husband of the Prophet's beloved daughter, Fatima. Ali ruled for about five years (AD 656–661), but his time was marked by great unrest among the faithful. Ali was more than just a companion of Muhammad; he was *family*, and some in Mecca believed that the leadership of Islam should remain that way forever. Others believed that it most definitely should not. Tension was in the air.

Groups loyal to Abu Bakr (that's *caliph* 1) and Uthman (*caliph* 3) rebelled against Ali, launching the first of several Muslim civil wars. The story gets more complicated at this point but the important thing to know is that one of the relatives of Uthman (*caliph* 3) emerged from this struggle as the leader of Islam (thus, becoming *caliph* number 5). The man's name was Muawiyah and he ruled (from Damascus in Syria, not Mecca in Saudi Arabia) for almost twenty years (AD 661–680). He elevated the *caliph* role to a kind of monarchy.

The next step in this story would split Islam in two to this very day. When Muawiyah (*caliph* 5) died, the role of *caliph* passed to his son, Yazid (*caliph* 6). However, those who thought the leadership of Islam should have remained in the family of the Prophet were outraged. They rallied around a man named Husayn, the son of Ali (*caliph* 4), and urged him to start a rebellion to win back the leadership of Islam for Muhammad's family. He tried, but was brutally slain in Karbala (central Iraq) in AD 680 by forces loyal to Yazid (*caliph* 6). According to the traditional accounts, Husayn's head was sent to Yazid as a trophy.

This event wrenched Islam in two forever. On the one side, you had those who accepted the leadership of *caliph* 6 (Yazid and his successors). On the other, you had those who insisted that after Ali (*caliph* 4) the leadership of Islam should have remained in the Prophet's family. The first group are the *Sunni*; the second are *Shi'ite*. These are the two great traditions within Islam today.

Sunni: traditional Islam

Sunnis ('traditionalists') may be regarded as those who follow a more orthodox path. About 85 per cent of today's Muslims are *Sunni*, so they have good reason for thinking of themselves as 'mainstream'. In line with this, *Sunnis* pride themselves on not being factional or interested in speculative sidetracks in theology. From their perspective, they just get on with the business of submitting to God's law as they perceive it.

One aspect of *Sunni* faith that highlights this self-awareness as 'majority' Islam is their view of how Islam should be governed. *Sunnis* were the ones, remember, who accepted the selection committee's decision about who should be *caliph*. In line with this, *Sunnis* today believe that matters of religious importance should be decided by a similar consensus (*ijma*). This is not exactly 'democracy' in the Western sense, since the 'consensus' referred to here is that of the *ulama*, or council of scholars. Final authority in *Sunni* Islam rests on the opinion of a special group of men expertly trained in the law (*Sharia*) of Islam.

Another tendency in *Sunni* Islam also goes back to the days of Ali (*caliph* 4), the son-in-law of Muhammad. When some were calling for the *caliph* role to remain in the Prophet's family the majority rejected what they saw as an excessive devotion to mere mortals. Ever since that time, *Sunni* Muslims have continued to display a similar aversion to (what they see as) 'superstition' – the veneration of Islamic 'saints', worship at Muslim shrines and tombs, and so on. *Sunnis* do have their own heroes and holy sites, but the mystical significance of these is less pronounced than in the second branch of Islam, *Shi'ite*.

Shi'ite: the party of Ali

Shi'ites are a minority group in Islam making up just 15 per cent of today's Muslims (though they are in the majority in countries like Iraq and Iran). The characteristic feature of this form of Islam is a deep passion for the memory of Muhammad, Fatima, Ali, and all the other members of the Prophet's family. Several things emerge from this devotion to the 'holy family'.

Shi'ites do not acknowledge the authority of the *Sunni* 'consensus of scholars'. This, of course, goes right back to the days following the death of Ali (*caliph* 4). *Shi'ites* then believed that only a member of the Prophet's family, such as Ali, or Ali's son, Husayn, should rule Islam. When Husayn was slain they turned to other members of the family to rule (their branch of) Islam. Each successive leader was called not a *caliph* (as in *Sunni* Islam) but an *Imam* ('leader'). These *Imams* were considered faultless in matters of doctrine and law. They were thought to be blessed with unusual closeness to Allah and could therefore even become an object of religious devotion.

There were twelve successive *Imams* in early *Shi'ite* history and all of them are now objects of veneration: their tombs are visited; their births and deaths are commemorated, and so on. These *Imams* are even thought to be able to intercede with Allah on behalf of the faithful. Whereas *Sunni* Muslims believe that a person is responsible for his or her own salvation, *Shi'ites* believe that the religious 'credit' of the great Imams can be passed on to the faithful here and now. Various aspects of *Shi'ite* practice are designed to access some of that credit.

Another interesting feature of *Shi'ite* faith is the belief that the twelfth *Imam*, who lived and disappeared in the ninth century, will reappear at the end of history. When he comes, *Shi'ites* say, he will restore justice to the world and establish Islam (*Shi'ite* Islam, of course) throughout the world. For now this *Imam* is hidden but Allah will reveal him in due course. He is therefore known as *Mahdi*, the 'expected one'.

At the heart of *Shi'ite* Islam is a belief in the glory of martyrdom. This, of course, goes back to the brutal slaying of Husayn, son of Ali (*caliph* 4). *Shi'ites* view this event as a symbol of the faith. They are the persecuted minority who must fight against the forces of evil whatever the cost. This point is reinforced each year in the great *Shi'ite* pilgrimage to Karbala in Iraq where Husayn was killed. Hundreds of thousands of Muslims travel there to re-enact the bloody events. By doing so, the faithful reaffirm their commitment to the family of the Prophet and rededicate themselves to the path of persecution and martyrdom. Doing so earns spiritual merit with Allah.

Fatima, the daughter of Muhammad (wife of Ali), is also an object of veneration in *Shi'ite* Islam. Like the *Imams* she is regarded as a mediator between God and humankind. She also exemplifies the virtues of womanhood and is a popular focus of devotion among *Shi'ite* women.

Sufism: mystical Islam

As Islam emerged as the major religion of Arabia and beyond (eighth–ninth centuries) the Islamic elite became increasingly vulnerable to the criticism of 'worldliness'. Their interest in power and possessions was viewed by some as a departure from true Islam. A tradition emerged in response to this worldliness that would eventually become a mass movement. It is called *Sufism*, the mystical branch of Islam.

The story of *Sufism* begins with a man named Hasan al-Basri (643–728). As a member of the *Sunni* council of scholars (the *ulama*) Hasan was part of the privileged class of Arabian society. He rejected power and wealth, however, preferring a life of discipline and simplicity. Hasan and others were Muslim 'ascetics', and they believed that the only way to cultivate true faith in God was to deny the false charms of the world. The word *sufi* derives from the Arabic word for 'wool': ascetics at the time were known to wear long woollen robes.

The next stage in the emergence of *Sufism* involved a woman named Rabia al-Adawiyya (late 700s). Rabia was a woman of extraordinary faith in Allah. She took the asceticism of Hasan and combined it with a more devotional approach to the worship of God. Her faith was not only about discipline and denial but also about *affection* for the Almighty. Consider these famous and beautiful words of Rabia:

> *O my Lord, if I worship You from fear of Hell, burn me in hell, and if I worship You in hope of Paradise, exclude me from there, but if I worship You for Your own sake, then withhold not from me Your Eternal Beauty (*Worship, *Rabia al-Adawiyya).*

This blend of monk-like discipline with emotional spirituality would set the character of *Sufism* from then on and launch *Sufism* into the mass market. By the AD 900s *Sufism* was thriving throughout the Islamic world.

The popular appeal of *Sufism* in the tenth–twelfth centuries could easily have brought its downfall. *Sufis* tended to bypass the hierarchy of Islam, believing you could create your own contact with God. As you might imagine, this was unacceptable to the traditional scholars of Islam whose role was to preserve and interpret the teachings of the Prophet without innovation and distortion. *Sufis* threatened this order and so became objects of persecution from mainstream Islamic leaders.

Sufism may well have been wiped off the face of the earth if it were not for the third person in the *Sufi* story, Abu Hamid al-Ghazali (1058–1111). Al-Ghazali was a hero of mainstream Islam. He was a scholar, lecturer and prolific writer. He had been particularly useful in the fight against Islamic heretics. Amongst the scholarly *ulama* (council) he was very highly regarded.

At the height of his fame, Al-Ghazali became strangely ill, losing the ability to speak. He withdrew from public life and found comfort – you guessed it – in *Sufism*. Al-Ghazali did what he did best: he wrote a book. In it he sought to demonstrate that traditional Islam fitted perfectly with the devotional and ascetic approach of *Sufism*. The book was a huge success, and it is credited with saving *Sufism* from possible extinction. From that point on, *Sufism* was regarded as a credible – if not always completely trusted – branch within mainstream Islam.

Several things characterize *Sufism* in modern Islam. First, there is a strong tendency amongst the *Sufis* to deny the pleasures of the world. This, they believe, is the only path to true knowledge of God. Related to this, secondly, is a commitment to 'poverty' as a way of life. Some *Sufis* belong to monastery-like communities in which they live simply and separately from society.

Thirdly, *Sufis* are known for their mystic devotion. Believers often spend hours in the study of the Koran (to find its hidden meanings), in prayer and in the repetition of sacred verses (from the Koran or sacred poetry). This is occasionally accompanied by breathing exercises reminiscent of Hindu yoga. Many historians believe *Sufism* was in fact influenced at some point by contact with Indian gurus. Connected with this mystical approach is the *Sufi* delight in sacred music. Some *Sufis* believe that singing and dancing (in a quite hypnotic manner) can lift you beyond yourself into an experience of oneness with God.

Fourthly, like *Shi'ites*, *Sufis* venerate certain dead and living 'saints' and regard these as mediators between God and humankind. Some *Sufi* groups have extended their mystical tendencies in quite extreme ways, advocating drunkenness and erotic behaviour as a means of experiencing the love and power of God. Needless to say, mainstream Islam looks on such 'superstition' with disdain.

This discussion of various types of Islam should not obscure the fact that Muslims of all varieties agree on the basics of the faith. These Islamic fundamentals are discussed in the next chapter.

25 The five pillars of Islam

The Koran and the example of the Prophet

Despite the heated disputes over how Islam should be ruled, Muslims have always agreed on where the *ultimate* authority lies.

Two things govern Muslim existence, whether in the seventh century or the twenty-first. First and foremost is the Koran, the very Word of God, according to Muslims. Second is the 'example' of the Prophet. The things Muhammad did and said in his life provide the model for Muslim living. This model is called the *Sunna* of the Prophet.

We saw earlier that the life of Muhammad is recorded in the *Hadiths*, or 'reports' about his words and deeds. Muslims do not regard these *Hadiths* as 'divinely inspired' in the way the Koran is, but the pattern of Muhammad's life contained in them is inspired. What the Prophet did and said, as narrated by the *Hadiths*, is considered infallible and binding on all believers. Two statements in the Koran itself guarantee the authority of Muhammad's example (*Sunna*):

Should you disagree about anything refer it to God and the Apostle [Muhammad], if you truly believe in God (4:59).

There is a good example [Sunna] in God's apostle for those of you who look to God (33:21).

Daily life for a Muslim is about doing the will of Allah. Knowledge of that will is found in the Koran and the *Sunna*.

In the Koran one hears the words of God; in Muhammad's example (*Sunna*) one sees the ways of God lived out.

It is now time to unpack Allah's will and talk about the major beliefs and practices of Islam as revealed in the Koran and the example of the Prophet.

Submission to God's law: the heart of Islam

You may have been wondering for the last 3,600 words what the word 'Islam' means. Unlike the word 'Hinduism', which gives away nothing about the religion of India, 'Islam' takes us to the very heart of the practice of Muslims. The term means simply *submission* and is a reference to surrendering your life to Allah. The related word 'Muslim' means *one who submits* (to Allah).

The term 'Islam' tells you something essential about the religion contained in the Koran (and the *Sunna*). The faith of the Muslim is a comprehensive *way of life* more than a wide-ranging *set of beliefs*. Muslims will often underline this. To be a Muslim, they point out, does not require belief in complex ideas such as the Trinity or the Five Aggregates of Attachment; one simply has to *submit* to the will of Allah. They will insist that their religion is more simple in a theological sense than, say, Christianity.

As a Christian I must admit there is some truth in this. Islam does have its own fixed set of beliefs (or 'dogma') but these are easier to get your head around than a doctrine like the Trinity.

What Islam 'lacks' in the complexity of its beliefs it amply makes up for in the extent of its laws. As any Muslim will tell you, the life of submission to Allah has implications for every area of life: what you eat, what you wear, when you pray, how much money you give away, and so on.

The central concept of the Muslim life is not 'faith' (as in Christianity) or 'enlightenment' (as in Buddhism) but *submission to God's law* as revealed in the Koran and in the example of Muhammad. That law is called *Sharia*, which literally means a 'path to a watering hole'. It is a lovely image really, implying a pathway through the desert to life-giving water. And this is exactly how Muslims see it. Surrendering yourself to God's *Sharia* leads to eternal Paradise. Disobedience to that law leads to destruction on the Day of Judgment.

All Muslims agree that the heart of the *Sharia* – this law leading to life-is found in just five simple practices. These are often called the 'Five Pillars of Islam' and every Muslim is obliged to obey them. By submitting to these five demands men and women hope to secure their place in Paradise.

First pillar: declaration of faith (shahada)

At least once in life every Muslim must confess out loud his or her belief in the twin essentials of Islam: the uniqueness of Allah as the only god, and the status of Muhammad as Allah's final Prophet. This confession is expressed in the words of the *shahada*, or official 'declaration' of the Muslim:

'There is no god but Allah; Muhammad is the Prophet of Allah.'

The declaration is simple, but it has to be made sincerely and with full knowledge of what it implies. This is where it gets a little more detailed.

Obviously, the first part of the declaration affirms 'monotheism', the belief that there is just one god. In its seventh-century context, this affirmation is set against both pagan 'polytheism' and Christian teachings about Jesus.

The first of these is obvious. Muhammad completely rejected the idol worship and polytheism of his native Mecca. One of his first acts when he took leadership of the city was to cleanse the *Kaba* (the box-like building housing the Meccan idols) and claim it for Allah. Actually, the Prophet believed he was reclaiming it, since tradition has it that the *Kaba* was originally built by Abraham (around 1800 BC). Abraham is believed to be the first true worshipper of Allah.

The statement 'There is no god but Allah' is set against Christian beliefs as much as pagan ones. We have already seen that Christians understood Jesus to be 'God in human form'.

For Muhammad though this involved an unacceptable association of a 'creature' (Jesus) with the 'Creator'. God in his greatness, insisted the Prophet, could never become subject to human weakness and mortality. Hence, the Christian doctrine of the 'incarnation' (God becoming human) was regarded as absurd. The Koran does not mince words about this:

> Unbelievers are those that say: 'God is the Messiah, the son of Mary.' For the Messiah himself said: 'Children of Israel, serve God, my Lord and your Lord.' He that worships other deities besides God, God will deny him Paradise, and the Fire shall be his home...Unbelievers are those that say: 'God is one of three.' There is but one God. If they do not desist from so saying, those of them that disbelieve shall be sternly punished... The Messiah, the son of Mary, was no more than an apostle: other apostles passed away before him. His mother was a saintly woman. They both ate earthly food (5:74–76).

The Koran accuses Christians of believing in three different gods – Allah, the Holy Spirit and Jesus. The absurdity of this belief is underlined in the statement that Jesus 'ate earthly food'. The Muslim picture of God, as eternal and majestic, completely rules out the idea of Him also being 'humble', lowering Himself to the point of needing to eat and drink.

When Muslims declare the first part of the *shahada* – 'There is no god but Allah' – they are self-consciously refuting both pagan and Christian ideas about God.

The second part of the Muslim's declaration of faith has to do with the status of their founder: 'Muhammad is the Prophet of Allah'. This statement has at least three implications for a Muslim. First, it expresses one's belief in the Koran as the Word of God. This is obvious, since the main evidence of Muhammad's prophetic activity was the Koran.

For Muslims the Koran is a miracle and 'proof' of the truth of Islam. Muhammad, they say, was illiterate and yet he was able to produce the finest piece of literature in the history of the world. Nothing approaches the Koran's literary quality, say Muslims. Its rhyme, rhythm and sheer acoustic beauty are unparalleled. Interestingly, this is not claimed for *translations* of the Koran (English or otherwise). Muslims believe that a translation of the Koran is not really a Koran at all. The true Koran was revealed to Muhammad *in Arabic* and was a copy of an original Arabic Koran kept in heaven. Having said this, if you cannot bring yourself to learn Arabic, believers would still urge you to read a translation of the Koran. Its truths, if not its full beauty, are apparent in any language, says the Muslim.

There is another implication of the declaration that 'Muhammad is the Prophet of Allah'. Implicit here is a commitment to the example (*Sunna*) of Muhammad. As we saw earlier, the words and deeds of the Prophet set the agenda of a Muslim's life. How could it be any other way? If Muhammad really was the chosen instrument of Allah, his pattern of life must embody God's ideal. Much of the motivation for a Muslim's daily conduct comes from a desire to emulate the great Prophet. Because of this, the stories of Muhammad's life contained in the *Hadiths* (reports) are extremely popular throughout the Muslim world.

The third implication of a Muslim's belief in 'Muhammad as the Prophet of Allah' is an awareness of his place in religious history. In particular, it involves an understanding of his connection with Jesus, Moses and Abraham, who were also Prophets (with a capital 'P').

Muslims believe that Allah did reveal himself to Abraham and Moses, but that the Jewish people twisted the original message into the teachings now contained in the Torah (or Old Testament). Only a dim reflection of the true revelation of Allah is still visible in the Jewish Scriptures, say modern Muslims.

The same applies to Jesus. Jesus was a great prophet sent by Allah to bring guidance to his people. His message, however, was soon forgotten, according to Muslims, and distorted into the religion reflected in the New Testament.

The Koran certainly has higher regard for Jews and Christians than for pagans. It calls the former 'people of the book', a phrase that affirms them as former recipients of God's revelation. If, however, one wants an unchanged, reliable account of God's truth, one must turn to the Koran, say Muslims. In one sense then the Koran is thought to 'confirm' the Scriptures of the Jews and Christians, endorsing those parts that do not contradict the Koran. In another sense, the Koran stands 'guard' over these Scriptures, correcting their perceived errors:

> *Evil-doers are those that do not judge according to God's revelations. And to you We have revealed the Book with the truth [the Koran]. It confirms the [Jewish and Christian] Scriptures which came before it and stands as a guardian over them. Therefore give judgement among men according to God's revelations, and do not yield to their [Jews and Christians] whims or swerve from the truth made known to you (5:47–48).*

In short, the statement, 'Muhammad is the Prophet of Allah', casts Muhammad as the final and authoritative Messenger of God in a long line of messengers whose original teachings were lost.

Making this 'declaration of faith' (the *shahada*) with a careful understanding of what it implies is the first and foundational pillar of Islam. It is the beginning of God's *Sharia*, his law leading to life.

Second pillar: daily prayer (salat)
The second 'pillar' of God's law is the obligation of daily prayer:

> *Recite your prayers at sunset, at nightfall, and at dawn; the dawn prayer has its witnesses. Pray during the night as well; an additional duty, for the fulfilment of which your Lord may exalt you to an honourable station (17:78).*

In Islam, prayer (*salat*) takes a slightly different form from that found in, say, Christianity. Christians tend to pray in an informal manner, bringing their daily needs to God, thanking him for various blessings in their lives, and so on. The prayers which Muslims are required to offer are what you might call *fixed* prayers. This is not to say Muslims do not also engage in informal prayers – many do – it is simply to point out that Islamic prayer is more ritualized and communal than that of many Christians.

Muslim prayers take place on five occasions during the day, reminding the faithful that they are dependent on Allah for all things at all times. The specific hours of prayer, and the body movements that go with each prayer are described in the example, or *Sunna*, of the Prophet. Muhammad prayed (and so now Muslims pray) at dawn, midday, mid-afternoon, sunset and evening every day of the year. Before each time of prayer a symbolic washing of the face, hands and feet also takes place. Sometimes water is used for this, sometimes dust or sand. This cleansing ritual prepares the worshipper to approach God.

During these prayers the worshipper will lie prostrate (with face to the ground) several times. This is always done in the direction of Mecca, the birthplace of the Prophet, and is intended to convey humility before the Creator. For Muslims, knowing that their brothers and sisters throughout the world are saying the same things, facing in the same direction, at the same times of the day, is a powerful reminder of the unity of the Islamic community.

In Muslim countries the times for prayer are announced throughout the city by the *muezzin*, an official of the mosque. He calls out (often through a large P.A. system):

God is most great (Allahu Akbar), God is most great, God is most great, I witness that there is no god but Allah; I witness that there is no god but Allah. I witness that Muhammad is His messenger. I witness that Muhammad is His messenger. Come to prayer, come to prayer. Come to prosperity, come to prosperity. God is most great. God is most great. There is no god but Allah.

Muslims may pray wherever they happen to be at the time – at the workplace, on the side of a road, at home, and so on. Only the Friday midday prayers are meant to be said with other Muslims in the local mosque. At that time, an official (often called the *imam*) usually gives a 'sermon' urging people to live in submission to Allah. Both men and women worship together at the mosque, but women usually do so in a separate section of the building (frequently behind a screen). This is designed not for sexist reasons but to avoid any awkwardness as worshippers (male or female) bend over and lie prostrate in front of each other.

What is said during these five daily prayers? Among the most important prayers is a recitation of the opening paragraphs of the Koran. The believer prays:

In the name of God, the compassionate, the most merciful. Praise be to God, Lord of the Universe, The Compassionate, the Merciful, Sovereign of the Day of Judgement! You alone we worship, and to You alone we turn for help. Guide us to the straight path, the path of those whom You have favoured, Not of those who have incurred Your wrath, Nor of those who have gone astray (1:1–7).

At the conclusion of the prayers the believer says the *shahada* (the declaration of faith mentioned earlier): 'There is no god but Allah; Muhammad is the Prophet of Allah.'

For Muslims prayer flows from and exemplifies the believer's desire to submit to Allah.

Third pillar: tax for the poor (zakat)

The third 'pillar' of Islam is both an act of worship toward God and an act of kindness toward fellow Muslims. It is the *zakat*, or poor-tax:

Attend to your prayers and render the alms levy (zakat). Whatever good you do shall be recompensed by God. God is watching all your actions (2:110).

I said earlier that one of the things that disturbed the pagan officials of Mecca about Muhammad was his preaching against their greed and selfishness. In this way, the Prophet was similar to Jesus and the Jewish prophets. Indeed, many scholars believe that the *zakat* of Islam derives from the Jewish (and Christian) practice of giving 'alms' for the poor. Most Muslims would reject this analysis. The notion of an Islamic tax came directly from Allah, say Muslims.

The *zakat* is usually calculated as an annual tax of about 2.5 per cent of a person's total wealth – both income and possessions. In Muslim countries such as Saudi Arabia the tax is strictly monitored by the state (sometimes it is absorbed into normal state taxes). In Western countries the tax is often collected through the mosque and is 'voluntary' in the sense that no one scrutinizes the amount you pay. This is left up to the conscience of the worshipper.

Where does the money collected via the *zakat* go? The Koran (2:72–74, 9:60) and *Sharia* law stipulate that the tax may be used for any or all of the following causes: for the relief of the poor and orphans, as a reward for volunteers in *jihad*-war, and for the spread of Islam throughout the world. In addition to the *zakat*, Muslims are urged by the Koran (and the example of the Prophet) to be generous to needy members of the *umma* (the Islamic 'community') wherever such are found. As I've said several times already, justice and charity toward one's Muslim brothers and sisters loom large in Islam:

> *The righteous man is he... who, though he loves it dearly, gives away his wealth to kinsfolk (2:177).*

Fourth pillar: the fast of Ramadan (sawm)

The fourth critical aspect of Muslim law is a month-long fast during Ramadan, the ninth month of the Islamic (lunar) calendar.

You may remember that it was during the month of Ramadan back in AD 610 that Muhammad is reported to have first heard the call of God to be the Prophet. It was the time when the 'recitation' (Koran) began to be revealed. This is what the fast of Ramadan is all about. It is a celebration of the marvel of God's revelation in the Koran:

> *In the month of Ramadan the Koran was revealed, a book of guidance for mankind with proofs of guidance distinguishing right from wrong. Therefore whoever of you is present in that month let him fast. But he who is ill or on a journey shall fast a similar number of days later on. God desires your well-being, not your discomfort. He desires you to fast the whole month so that you may magnify God and render thanks to Him for giving you His guidance (2:184–185).*

The point of the fast is clear: it is all about praising Allah for his mercy in giving mankind the 'guidance' we need to walk in God's paths.

The fast of Ramadan begins when an official announces the sighting of the full moon (hence, a cloudy night sky can postpone the fast for a day). At this announcement, every Muslim abstains (during daylight hours) from food, drink and sexual activity for the entire month. Families usually enjoy an early breakfast together just before sunrise. This has to keep them going until sunset when they can enjoy another meal together.

On the twenty-seventh day of the month Muslims celebrate the night they believe Muhammad first heard the angelic voice. It is called the 'Night of Power', for obvious reasons. The fast comes to an end a couple of days later with – not surprisingly – a huge feast. It is called the 'Feast of the Breaking of the Fast' and it is a time of great joy, equivalent perhaps to Christmas for people in the West. Many Muslims take the opportunity at this time to exchange gifts, mindful always of the greater 'gift' that is the Koran.

Fifth pillar: pilgrimage to Mecca (Hajj)

The final 'pillar' of Islam may seem to us a little burdensome. Muslims would disagree, however, describing it as one of the greatest privileges of their life. Every Muslim adult who is physically and financially able must make a pilgrimage (at least once in life) to the birthplace of the Prophet, to Mecca in Saudi Arabia:

> *Exhort all (Muslim) men to make the pilgrimage. They will come to you on foot and on the backs of swift camels from every distant quarter; they will come to avail themselves of many a benefit, and to pronounce on the appointed days the name of God over the cattle which He has given them for food. Eat of their flesh, and feed the poor and the unfortunate. Then let the pilgrims tidy themselves, make their vows, and circle the Ancient House (the Kaba). Such is God's commandment. He that reveres the sacred rites of God shall fare better in the sight of his Lord (22:27–30).*

During his life Muhammad made numerous trips to Mecca, where he worshipped his God in the very place he believed Abraham had worshipped God 2,500 years before. The fact that this lengthy pilgrimage is now obligatory for all (able) believers shows just how seriously Muslims take the idea of imitating the example (*Sunna*) of their Prophet.

Nowadays, the *Hajj* is a logistical miracle, with over two million people each year descending on the Saudi Arabian city for up to a fortnight. The festival takes place during the twelfth month of the Islamic year (Dhil-Hijja) and officially lasts for six days.

Several rituals are performed by worshippers during the pilgrimage. First, dressed in white sheets as a symbol of purity, pilgrims make their way to the *Kaba*. You may remember that Muhammad 'cleansed' the *Kaba* when he took over Mecca in AD 629. He removed its idols and reclaimed it for the One true God. Because of this, the building is a symbol of the statement: 'There is no god but Allah.' On arriving at the *Kaba*, which is situated in the middle of the Great Mosque, pilgrims walk around the structure seven times. This is a picture of the way a Muslim's life revolves around Allah. The court of the Great Mosque where all this happens can apparently squeeze in more than a quarter of a million worshippers at one time. That's one big building.

Another essential part of the *Hajj* itinerary includes spending an afternoon and evening on the plain of Arafat, near where Muhammad gave his farewell sermon to the Meccans. From midday until sunset pilgrims call out to Allah for mercy. Many Muslims believe that this part of the *Hajj* will wash away all previously committed sins. A believer is able to leave this ritual a new person, forgiven by God for past sins. I once heard a Muslim describe this experience as being 'born again'. I heard another Muslim confess his hope that attending this Arafat ritual would earn salvation for his father who had died prior to performing the *Hajj* for himself. Such is the power of these rituals for modern Muslims.

Another (more minor) ritual associated with the *Hajj* involves throwing pebbles at large stone pillars. This is known as 'stoning the devil', and it is a way for believers to show their hatred for the forces of evil. People are frequently injured during this ritual because the 'throwing' can get quite vigorous and the pebbles quite large.

The *Hajj* concludes with the Feast of Sacrifice. Goats and sheep are sacrificed *en masse* in remembrance of Abraham's sacrifice millennia before. Some of the meat is then eaten by worshippers and the rest, in keeping with Islamic charity, is distributed to the poor. The freezing, packaging and delivery of these leftovers requires another display of logistical brilliance on the part of the Saudi government.

On returning from the *Hajj* pilgrims will usually feel more confident of their standing before God. They will also experience a deepened resolve to *submit* to Allah in the year to come. Some will complete the *Hajj* many times in their life; others will do it just once, and still others may never experience it at all. Either way, this great pilgrimage remains one of the five minimum acts of obedience to Islamic law (*Sharia*).

The law of Islam (in the Koran and the example of the Prophet) covers many other parts of life: pork and alcohol are forbidden; modesty of dress is encouraged; inheritance laws are strictly regulated, and so on. The Five Pillars, however, capture the heart of that law (*Sharia*). Submitting to these five demands ensures God's favour, say both *Sunni* and *Shi'ite* Muslims. It makes one ready for the Day of Judgment when Allah will reward the righteous.

Islam in brief

Life of Muhammad
- Born AD 570
- Called to be 'Prophet' / Koran revealed in AD 610
- Flees to Medina in AD 622 (beginning of Muslim calendar)
- Takes back Mecca in AD 629
- Dies AD 632

Types of Islam
- *Sunni*: majority 'traditional' Islam
- *Shi'ite*: dedicated to Muhammad's family (via Ali)
- *Sufi*: mystical branch of Islam

Sources of Islamic faith
- Koran: the very Word of God (in Arabic)
- *Sunna*: the example of the Prophet (recorded in the *Hadiths*)

Five Pillars of Islam (the heart of Muslim Sharia, or 'law')
1. The declaration of faith (*shahada*): one God; Muhammad is the Prophet
2. Prayer (*salat*): five times a day; together at the mosque on Fridays
3. Tax for the poor (*zakat*): 2.5% for the underprivileged and the spread of Islam
4. The fast of *Ramadan* (*sawm*): month-long commemoration of the coming down of the Koran
5. Pilgrimage to Mecca (*Hajj*): journey to the birthplace of the Prophet; believed to wash away the Muslim's past sins

Facts and figures on Islam today
- Islam is the *second* largest religion in the world with over one billion believers.[1]
- Muslims make up about 20% of the world's population.[2]
- Islam is found in more than 200 countries worldwide.[3]
- Around three million Muslims make the trip to Mecca each year.

• Some countries operate schemes to help people pay for the *Hajj*. In Malaysia there is a lottery with first prize being an all expenses paid pilgrimage to Mecca.

[1, 2, 3] *Britannica Book of the Year 2004*, Encyclopaedia Britannica Inc. (p 280)

Famous Muslims include:
Malcolm X (1925–65)
Assassinated leader of 'Nation of Islam' movement in the USA. Known for struggle for civil rights for black Americans.

Muhammad Ali
World champion boxer – changed his name from Cassius Clay.

Imran Khan
Pakistani cricketer (1971–92), Oxford scholar and currently politician in Pakistan.

Nusrat Feteh Ali Khan (1948–97)
Nusrat Feteh Ali Khan was a singer of Qawaali – a style of Islamic *Sufi* singing. He claimed that Allah called him to become a singer at the age of thirty. He sang with Pearl Jam's Eddie Vedder on the soundtrack to *Dead Man Walking* in 1995. Has the *Guinness Book of Records* entry for the biggest recording output by Qawaali artist – 125 albums.

Good books and sites on Islam today
http://www.islam.com
(comprehensive links to all things Islamic)

http://www.usc.edu/dept/MSA/reference/searchhadith.html
(a site for searching all of the *Hadiths* about Muhammad)

Esposito, J. L., *Islam: the Straight Path*. Oxford: Oxford University Press, 1998.

Rodinson, R., *Muhammad*. New York: The New Press, 2002.

Clarke, P., 'Islam: Introduction', in *The World's Religions* (ed. S. Sutherland, et al.). London: Routledge, 1988, 307–312.

Baldick, J., 'Early Islam', in *The World's Religions* (ed. S. Sutherland, et al.). London: Routledge, 1988, 313–328.

Beckerlege, G. (ed.), *World Religions Reader* (2nd edition). London: Routledge, 2001 (*Part Three: Islam*, 127–198).

Dawood, N. J. (translator), *The Koran*. London: Penguin Books, 2003.

Smart, N. and Hecht, R. (editors), 'Islam', in *Sacred Texts of the World: a universal anthology*. New York: Crossroad, 2002, 125–177.

Smart, N., *The World's Religions* (2nd edition). Cambridge: Cambridge University Press, 2003, 285–306.

Letting the religions have their say

26 What's wrong with Jesus

No dimming the lights

The title of this chapter is perhaps the opposite of what you might expect from a writer claiming to be a follower of Christ. Surely, a Christian author would want to explain what's wrong with Hinduism, Islam, Judaism and Buddhism! It is true, as I mentioned in chapter two, that many books from the Christian stable set out to do just that. There are numerous Islamic critiques of the world religions as well.

But my title is deliberate. Critiquing non-Christian religions has not been even a minor aim of this book. I said at the outset that I wanted to approach the great Faiths as works of art worthy of display in the best light. I have tried to help readers – Christian or otherwise – to understand and appreciate where the vast religious majority of the world is coming from.

This is not to say that I think critiquing the Faith of others is invalid *per se*. Not at all. But I do believe such a thing is inappropriate (and virtually impossible) without first attempting to see what others see in their religion. Put another way, until I am able to answer a question like, 'Why are millions of people attracted to Buddhism?' I am in no position to evaluate the Buddha's teachings.

As I said in the Introduction to the book, dimming the lights on Hinduism, Buddhism, Judaism and Islam, and then turning them up on Christianity could never be an expression of sincere Christian commitment. It would in fact be an indication of my own uncertainty about Christianity. If I need to obscure other traditions in order to make my own look good, I clearly don't trust Christ's capacity to hold his own in the 'art gallery' of the Faiths. In reality, I am more than ever convinced of the unique truthfulness and beauty of Christ amidst the world religions. And I could think of no better way to express that confidence than to turn the lights on full and let you browse the entire collection for yourself.

'They all look the same to me'

Another benefit of turning the lights up full, so to speak, is that it allows readers to observe the very real differences between the great religions of the world. As I said in chapter 2, it has become increasingly fashionable in our society to emphasize just how *similar* the world Faiths are: 'they all speak about a Higher Power and about being nice to each other. Let's just leave it at that.'

But stressing the sameness of the world's religions gives honour to none of them. Imagine attending an art exhibition of the classical masters, turning the lights down low, standing at a distance, and declaring: 'They all look pretty much the same to me.' To give a musical example, imagine someone's grandma attending a rock festival, listening to all the bands from the back of the crowd with her fingers in her ears, and then announcing authoritatively: 'They all sound the same to me.'

The only way to pay our respect to different traditions – whether artistic, musical, or religious – is to look closely at them, listen carefully to their emphases, and allow them to convey their different perspectives. Once we've done that for a while it becomes perfectly clear that, while many of the religions are superficially alike, most of them are fundamentally different.

Why religions are different

There are at least three reasons for the differences between the world religions. Firstly, some of the Faiths ask similar questions but arrive at radically different answers. Buddhists and Hindus, for example, both ask: how can I escape this physical world? The answers they come up with couldn't be further apart.

Secondly, because of the different cultural backgrounds of the religions, several of them are not even asking the same questions. For example, the Christian question, 'How can I find favour with the Creator?' does not even register on the Buddhist radar. Without asking the same questions it is difficult to arrive at the same conclusions.

The third reason for the differences between the religions is the most obvious. Several of the great Faiths rose partly in reaction to the perceived errors of what came before. Buddha's teaching, you may remember, was set deliberately against his native Hinduism. The rabbis of Classical Judaism framed their traditions in conscious denial of the 'heresies' of the Essenes, Sadducees and Christians. Islam, furthermore, saw the Koran as God's final account of a truth that had been lost and corrupted by Jews and Christians.

I want now to outline some of the most striking differences between the religions of the world. The careful reader will have spotted these along the way, but a brief run-down of them here in the conclusion to the book I think will help us honour the religions by appreciating what is distinctive about them.

One way to draw attention to these differences would be to unpack what Christianity finds 'wrong' with the other Faiths. I want to do the opposite. In what follows I hope to show what is 'wrong' with Christianity from the perspective of Hinduism, Buddhism, Judaism and Islam-hence the title of this chapter. I am not trying to be clever here, and I am certainly not trying to upset my fellow Christians. I want only to demonstrate clearly, and in a fair way, the sheer diversity of opinion that exists among the religions of the world.

What's wrong with Jesus: Hinduism

Let me begin with Hinduism. Perhaps the most obvious inadequacy in Christianity, from the Hindu perspective, is its belief about the future kingdom of God. Central to Hinduism, of course, is the doctrine of reincarnation – beings are trapped in a circle of rebirths until they merge with *Brahman*. Jesus, however, taught that every individual would face God's judgment after death. This would strike the average Hindu as a complete misreading of some of the fundamental realities of the universe.

The physical nature of the kingdom Jesus envisaged is also highly problematic. Jesus believed that at the Judgment the faithful would experience a resurrection from the dead (modelled on his own) and eternal life in a 'new creation'. For Hinduism, though, liberation (*moksha*) is precisely liberation from individual bodily existence into the non-bodily unity of *Brahman*. What could be more different!

Perhaps equally troublesome to Hindus is Jesus' claim to be the unique Son of God. Hindus are usually happy to include Jesus as another incarnation of one of the gods (Vishnu, Siva), but the idea that he is the singular human manifestation of the one true God is untenable within Hinduism's worldview. Finally, Jesus' teaching about grace runs counter to Hindu notions of human responsibility. Whereas Jesus taught that sins can be forgiven by God's pure mercy, the doctrine of *karma* (in its Hindu form) insists that sinful actions must reap their appropriate consequences. Grace and *karma* are entirely at odds at this point.

What's wrong with Jesus: Buddhism

I have said before that Buddhism has several problems with Hindu belief, most notably, with the existence of the soul/self (*atman*) and the necessity of divine sacrifice and worship. The differences between Buddhism and Christianity are just as real. Siddhartha Gautama would have shared Hinduism's scorn at the idea of a future bodily resurrection in a new creation. It is difficult to overstate just how radically different the Eastern (Hinduism, Buddhism) and Western (Judaism, Christianity, Islam) visions of eternal reality are.

In addition, Jesus' insistence that humanity's deepest need was forgiveness of sins would have struck Buddha as a deep ignorance born of the twin illusions that (a) there is a Self who sins and (b) there is a Creator who forgives. The Buddhist writers I have read stress this point: Buddhism is not about guilt and mercy. It is about ignorance and enlightenment.

Christianity teaches that because men and women have rejected their Maker they lack the resources within themselves either to be truly good or even to know ultimate truth. These things must be received as gifts from God. This would have struck Buddha as a cop-out. It also flatly contradicts the important Theravada doctrine that human beings possess everything they need to be both pure and wise. No divine assistance is possible or necessary, says the Theravadin Buddhist. Even the Mahayana tradition – with its many deities and saviour figures – teaches that *Bodhisattvas* (Buddhas-to-be) must ultimately merit their attainment of Buddha status.

Another quite obvious problem with Jesus, from the Buddhist perspective, is his passion. One of the striking things about the Gospels is that Jesus is deeply moved by so many things. He weeps at the death of a friend; he is outraged at the hypocrisies of the temple officials (even overturning their tables and chairs), and he experiences fear and anguish at his impending death. Jesus' emotions became an important point of theological reflection in early Christianity. From the Buddhist perspective, however, Jesus' emotional reaction to his circumstances is completely at odds with the ideal taught by Siddhartha Gautama. Fear, anguish, anger, and so on, are the responses of someone captivated by 'desire'. Detachment and tranquility are the characteristics of the wise person, for the enlightened know that the Self does not exist and that *dukkha* (suffering) is only a creation of the ignorant striving after pleasure, existence and non-existence.

What's wrong with Jesus: Judaism

What about Judaism: what is wrong with Jesus from the Jewish point of view? At one level, Judaism and Christianity have the most in common of all the religions. They share a belief in God's promises to Abraham and King David. They view God as both Creator and Redeemer. They think of humanity as sinful and in need of divine mercy. They hold similar visions of the future messianic kingdom (Reform Judaism aside). They even share part of their Scriptures (the *Tanak* / Old Testament). For no other two religions is it true to say (at least in theory): 'They worship the same God.'

At another level, though, no two religions are more directly incompatible with each other than Judaism and Christianity. Perhaps the most basic tenet of Christianity is that Jesus is the 'Christ' (Hebrew: *Messiah*), the Anointed One sent by God in fulfilment of the Old Testament. For Jews, of course, Jesus was nothing of the sort. The Talmud sums up the official Jewish position on the matter: 'Jesus of Nazareth was hung up on the day of preparation for the Passover for practising sorcery and leading Israel astray' (*Baraita Sanhedrin* 43a). Around AD 100 the classical rabbis pronounced a curse on the Christians, describing them as 'heretics', 'enemies of God', and 'without hope' in God's kingdom. The curse is repeated to this day in the regular Orthodox and Conservative synagogue service (*Shemoneh Esrei* 12). Modern Jews in no way intend this as a personal insult against Christians, but the presence of this statement in the Jewish prayer book, or *Siddur*, is a daily reminder that, for all their shared heritage, Jews and Christians are poles apart on the small question of the Messiah!

What's wrong with Jesus: Islam

What about Islam's critique of Christianity? An article in the *Sydney Morning Herald* a few years ago tried to argue that Christians and Muslims really share an affection for the same Jesus. The piece was titled, 'The Love that Crosses the Great Divide', and in it the journalist rightly explained that the Jesus mentioned in the Koran is:

> ... not the Jesus who was the Son of God, admittedly, and who was crucified, but certainly the Jesus who was Messiah and miracle worker, who conversed regularly with God, who was born of a virgin and who ascended into heaven (24 Dec 2001).

If Muslims and Christians could just focus on *this* Jesus, argued the writer, they would experience a 'love that crosses the great divide'. I laughed out loud when I first read this article. The journalist was somehow unaware that all he was doing was asking Christians to 'halve' the Jesus they see in the New Testament and settle on the one described in the Koran. Let's be honest: a Jesus who was neither Son of God nor died on a cross is not the Christian Jesus. I am all for crossing the divide between religions and cultures, but I doubt very much that this is going to happen by Christians giving up their Jesus for the Muslim one.

It must be understood that according to Islamic theology a Prophet such as Jesus could never have suffered a fate as awful as Roman crucifixion: Allah would not have allowed it. The Koran says explicitly:

> *They did not kill Jesus, nor did they crucify him, but they thought they did... they knew nothing about him that was not sheer conjecture (Koran 4:157).*

It is tempting to dismiss this discrepancy as a small one. Christians might beg to differ: their entire faith is premised on the death and resurrection of Jesus. Muslims would also object. The Koran, by definition, contains no errors of history, ritual or belief. The Koran is not a historical source that can be measured against other historical sources; it is God's word, revealed directly from heaven. If this paragraph of the Koran were incorrect (unthinkable to a Muslim), the entire revelation would be suspect. But for Muslims the divine origin of their holy book guarantees the factual nature of every statement in it. Therefore, Jesus did not – could not have – died upon a cross. That is what is wrong with (the Christian) Jesus.

Muslims are even more concerned about what they see as the illogical Christian belief that Jesus is *one* with God. In chapter 25 I quoted section 5:74–76 of the Koran, which strenuously refutes the divinity of Christ. I remember once speaking at a university in Sydney on the theme of God's entry into the world as Jesus. A very polite and articulate Muslim man in the audience advised me during the question time that my lecture was 'blasphemous' from the Islamic perspective. He explained that to associate anything human with the Creator was a grave sin. I assured him I meant no offence, and the conversation ended amicably. It brought home to me – and to the slightly uncomfortable audience – just how different the Islamic and Christian pictures of God are. For the Christian, the idea that God entered our world and gave his life for us is perhaps the most beautiful mystery of the Faith. But what appears beautiful and mysterious to the Christian proves blasphemous and irrational to the Muslim.

An additional criticism that Islam levels against Christianity has to do with the Christian doctrine of *grace* discussed in chapter 20. Similar to Buddhism, Islam insists that human beings have the capacity to act in full accordance with the Truth. It also insists that it is the individual's responsibility to do so. Completely unacceptable then is Christianity's claim that salvation is a divine gift made possible only because of the work of Christ on our behalf (his death for our sins). Over the years I have discussed this point with numerous Muslim brothers, and all of them have insisted on the same thing: the New Testament emphasis on grace through Christ's atoning death robs Allah (and mankind) of due glory. Allah, they assure me, has revealed the effective path of salvation (the Five Pillars of Islam), and men and women are obliged and able to walk it.

Further differences between the world Faiths could be explored. In fact I suspect we could easily devote four more chapters to exploring 'What's wrong with Hinduism, Buddhism, Judaism and Islam'. For the reality is: all of the world's religions have significant 'issues' with all of the others. I point this out not because I want to start an argument between the religions – far from it – but because, it seems to me, when we say 'all Faiths teach the same things', we are doing a real disservice both to our own brains and to the religions themselves. I can't help feeling that the only way to say such a thing with a straight face is either to remain unaware of what the religions teach, which is perhaps bad for us, or to deliberately minimize their distinctive features, which is probably unfair to them.

27 Is it all ducks and rabbits?

The promise of 'pluralism'

Most people who look closely at the world religions stop repeating the fashionable mantra: 'All religions are the same.' The more acquainted you get with the Faiths, the more apparent their unique claims become.

Having said that, there is a more sophisticated logic open to those who want to keep affirming the ultimate unity of the world's religions. It is a logic that is becoming increasingly popular. I am talking about what is often called 'pluralism', the belief that spiritual truth is *plural* in form not singular.

The popular version of pluralism says, 'The religions are simply different paths up the same mountain' or 'All roads lead to Rome, and all religions lead to God' (except in the case of Theravada Buddhism which doesn't actually believe in God).

'Pluralism' is a powerful point of view, and whether or not you've heard the term I'm sure you have come across the viewpoint. Many readers may even share the pluralist perspective themselves. In this final chapter I want to outline the allure and strengths of pluralism before explaining what seem to me to be its inconsistencies and embarrassments. Ultimately, I suspect pluralism delivers less than it promises, both intellectually and personally.

The big Truth and little falsehoods

Sophisticated pluralists are fully aware of the contradictions between many of the beliefs of the great Faiths. But they respond to these discrepancies by saying that, although there are few *explicit* truths common to the world religions, there is a deeper, grander TRUTH made clear by them all.

What is this profound macro-truth? Well, it has little to do with things like Allah requiring five daily prayers, or Buddha advocating the removal of desire, or Jesus dying for the sins of the world. These 'truths' are just culturally specific *versions* of the greater truth that there is some indefinable REALITY drawing the world toward itself. Here is the ultimate religious dogma, according to pluralism: something Infinite calls us finite beings above and beyond ourselves.

Chris McGillion is a lecturer at Charles Sturt University, Australia, and the religious affairs columnist for my local newspaper, *The Sydney Morning Herald*. He provides a first-rate example of the sophisticated pluralist. In an article titled 'Groping at shadows in a darkened room', he wrote:

> *The very diversity of religions… speaks to a truth – that all people in every time and place have felt the need to respond to the infinite… The various religious traditions are the 'how' of that response… All religions are truthful in far more important ways than some of their propositions are false (18 March 2003).*

McGillion draws a distinction here between small propositions and the larger truth. The propositions, presumably, are things like Allah's call for prayer, Buddha's doctrine of detachment and Jesus' atoning death. The big truth, on the other hand, is simply that people 'have felt the need to respond to the infinite'. According to McGillion, the small propositions are probably false but at least the big idea is really true. This is what the logic of pluralism involves – an acceptance of the *sentiment* of religion but a denial of the *beliefs* of religion.

In academic circles, probably the most influential champion of pluralism over the last two decades is Professor John Hick of the University of Birmingham. For Professor Hick, religions are not *revelations* of spiritual Reality; they are simply *responses* to that Reality in a specific cultural situation. Individual religions are therefore to be thought of as 'signposts' to

Something they do not actually grasp themselves.

Exactly how Hick and others know this is never actually discussed in the literature on pluralism. The point is merely affirmed and illustrated with something resembling religious zeal. We are meant simply to believe that these few academic pluralists have discovered *the* truth which none of the great religious leaders of the past had been able to see for themselves. I'll say more about that in a moment.

The duck-rabbit experiment

In one of his books called *The Rainbow of Faiths* Professor Hick brilliantly explains his point of view by asking readers – as I'll ask you now – to look closely at a famous sketch first used by psychologists in early experiments on optical illusions:

As you can see, the sketch shows an ambiguous figure drawn to look like a duck (facing left) and a rabbit (facing right). Give yourself a moment to see both.

Now imagine conducting the following experiment. If you showed this picture to people who knew ducks but had never seen rabbits, what would they see? Obviously, a duck. If you showed it to a group that had seen rabbits but not ducks, they of course would see a rabbit.

Which group is correct, asks John Hick: the duck group or the rabbit group? Both are correct, he says. Both groups are entirely justified in describing this image variously as a duck or a rabbit. The 'contradiction' between the opinions is a matter of perception rather than substance.

So far, so good.

John Hick then compares religious truth with this optical illusion. He says that the great religions of the world contain merely perceptions of Reality rather than actual descriptions of Reality. Each perspective is culturally determined. Just as the duck-knowing group could only see a duck and the rabbit-knowing group a rabbit, so Muslims see Allah, Hindus see *Brahman* and Christians see the Trinity. No one is 'wrong'. It is just a cultural perception. It is all 'ducks' and 'rabbits'.

When I first read Professor Hick's argument I felt it was compelling. It seemed to provide what so many of us would like: a way of affirming all religions as true despite their apparent contradictions. Each religion could be a valid 'perception' of Reality without actually possessing that Reality.

But then something dawned on me that completely changed my mind. What John Hick does not make explicit is that there is actually a third party in this duck-rabbit analogy. There is not just the duck-knowing group and the rabbit-knowing group; there is also the person conducting the experiment. And that person *does* know the truth. In reality, the picture is not a sketch of a duck or a rabbit. It is actually an image drawn to look like both a duck *and* a rabbit. The unknowing subjects in the experiment may be justified in merely having a perception of the picture, but the person showing the image is under no such illusion. He knows full well that the sketch is a trick, carefully designed to produce what psychologists call 'rival-schemata ambiguity' – an illusion.

Without realizing it, John Hick's analogy succeeds in exposing an embarrassing, and rarely admitted, assumption of the pluralist point of view. Pluralism patronizingly suggests that although the world religions are each entitled to their *perceptions* of Reality (believing in Christ, Buddha, etc.), the truth of the situation, apparently known only to the pluralist, is that this Reality is ultimately unknowable, and that all religious perceptions are in fact illusions. In Professor Hick's analogy, then, the hidden assumption is that pluralists are like the ones conducting the experiment. They are the only ones 'in the know'.

Pluralism ends up claiming to have discovered a greater truth that none of the religions has observed before, and then it suggests that the 'lesser truths' individual religions thought they could see are in fact cultural illusions – just ducks and rabbits. This is a big call. By describing religions as true in a manner none of them has affirmed before and false in all the ways they have always affirmed, pluralism assumes an intellectual high ground that is positively breathtaking.

The presumption of pluralism

It is true of course that most of the religions also claim to possess a set of truths that others do not have. Buddhism claims this, Islam claims this, Christianity claims this, and so on. But three things make the claim of pluralism significantly more presumptuous than the claims of the world religions.

For starters, the world religions generally don't take credit for the discovery of their truths. For the most part, the great Faiths insist that a power greater than themselves *revealed* the truths which are by nature beyond human discovery. This is certainly true of Hinduism, Judaism, Christianity and Islam, all of which emphasize divine revelation. Pluralists, on the other hand, take all the credit for their insights themselves. Through their own intellect and imagination they have apparently discovered the macro-truth that relativizes all the religious micro-truths.

Secondly, when people from a world religion claim to possess truth (revealed from above) they do so in the knowledge that vast numbers of others also belong to this circle of truth. When a Muslim says, 'Allah has revealed himself in the Koran', he or she is including about a billion other people in the club. Likewise, when a Christian says, 'God can be seen in Christ's life, death and resurrection', he or she is including around two billion others. On the other hand, when pluralists like Chris McGillion say, 'All religions are truthful in far more important ways than some of their propositions are false' (*SMH* 18 March 2003), they do so aware that only a small number of other people actually embrace this truth. The tiny club of Western intellectual pluralists have discerned a Truth that is apparently 'far more important' than the little falsehoods of the vast religious majority of the world. This is presumption indeed.

There is a third reason pluralism is more presumptuous than any of the claims of the world religions. Pluralism makes its bold claim without even attempting to justify its premise. Let me explain.

I said earlier that writers such as John Hick insist that individual religions are merely *responses* to a Reality that is ultimately unknowable and out of their reach. I have always wanted to ask Hick and others two questions:

1. How do you know that no particular religion grasps Reality itself?

2. How do you know that this Reality is unknowable and out of reach?

Answers to these questions are never offered in the literature on the subject. And so my point is: when a claim this far-reaching is asserted without justification, it amounts to a special kind of presumption.

The closest Professor Hick comes to offering a 'reason' for pluralism is when he describes how intolerable he finds the alternative. Believing that only one religion is true, he says, consigns too many people to error (and possibly to hell, in the view of some religions). This is unthinkable. The far more bearable position, Hick believes, is to think of religions as all connected to Reality but incapable of accurately describing it. This is the more tolerable position and therefore the one that should be adopted.

Personally, I don't think pluralism does avoid unbearableness. As I've already argued, pluralism might not consign anyone to hell (since pluralists don't believe in hell), but it does consign virtually every religious tradition (except pluralism) to large-scale error. Leaving that aside, however, even if pluralism were more 'bearable' than the alternatives, since when has bearableness been a rational basis for accepting something as true? Plenty of unbearable things are true (such as: 90 per cent of the world's wealth is in the hands of 10 per cent of the world's people). Bearableness might provide a *motivation* for adopting pluralism but it does not provide a justification for doing so.

Whatever one thinks of the various beliefs of the world religions, at least when religious people make their claims they do so on some prior basis. The view that God requires five daily prayers is not simply the Muslim's preferred opinion; it is a belief, holds the Muslim, based on the authority of the perfect word of God, the Koran. Again, the view that Jesus died for the sins of the world is not just the Christian's favourite idea; it is a conviction, holds the Christian, based on the reliability of Christ's life, miracles, death and resurrection.

You and I might not share the Muslim's confidence in the Koran, or the Christian's confidence in the events of Jesus, but nor could we dismiss what the Muslim or Christian believes as baseless assertion. Pluralism is not so fortunate.

Economy of effort

The world religions clearly do not teach the same things. Some of their most important beliefs stand in stark contradiction to beliefs held dearly by others. Even the more sophisticated attempt of 'pluralism' fails ultimately to demonstrate that religions can be viewed as *one* (sharing equally in a 'truth' bigger than all their falsehoods).

So, why the trend in our society toward embracing these views? Why is it that we want to think that 'religions teach the same things', or that they are simply 'different paths up the same mountain'?

One motivation is surely the fear that religious conviction will lead to religious intolerance and, as a consequence, to discrimination and violence. The fear is understandable, isn't it? History is littered with examples of violent intolerance on the part Christians, Hindus, etc. And those of us who belong to a religious tradition, I believe, need to respond to our society's critique at this point by working harder at being more tolerant of one another.

By 'tolerant' I do not mean that we should accept each other's beliefs as *true*. That of course is impossible. A Buddhist, for instance, cannot accept as true both Siddhartha's doctrine of No-Soul and the Hindu doctrine of the soul. Again, a Jew cannot accept as true both the Orthodox hope for a future Messiah and the Christian belief that the Messiah has already lived, died and been raised to life.

No. By 'tolerance' I do not mean mere acceptance of other people's *beliefs*; I mean acceptance of *people* who hold contrary beliefs. This is true tolerance: the admirable ability to treat with friendship and respect those with whom you disagree. That is what religious people need, and in bucket loads!

I think there is an even stronger factor influencing our move toward pluralism and our avoidance of all discussion about the differences between the great Faiths. It has to do with the long-held Australian tradition of choosing the easier of two options. Some call it 'apathy'; I would rather call it 'economy of effort'.

Let me borrow an illustration from one of my previous books (*If I Were God I'd Make Myself Clearer*), with apologies to those who have read it.

Suppose you were to ask two Chinese friends how to say 'I love you' in Mandarin. One of them replies 'Wo ai ni''; the other says, 'Wo hen ni''. You now have a problem, which can be resolved in one of two ways. You could research the issue – speak to another Chinese friend, look up the entry in an English-Mandarin Dictionary, and so on. This will take a little effort but at least, in the end, you could make an informed decision. The other option is far easier. Rather than dwell on the discrepancy between the two answers, you could just assume that both are correct: perhaps they are different ways of saying the same thing, dialect variations of one original expression.

Affirming both answers as true will not only avoid upsetting anyone, it will require no effort on your part whatsoever. It's the perfect economy of effort – except that, in reality, 'Wo hen ni' means 'I hate you'!

I'm sure you can see the point.

When a Hindu affirms the existence of many personal deities and a Jew insists on the existence of just one, it produces a dilemma that can be approached in one of two ways. On the one hand, you could investigate for yourself the historical and philosophical arguments for polytheism versus monotheism. This might involve reading a book or two on the subject, or perhaps just getting alone and thinking the issue through. Alternatively, you could take the simpler option and affirm both claims as valid in their own way: there are both many gods *and* just one God. While this might pose a mathematical problem for some, it is clearly the path of least resistance.

Again, when a Buddhist or Muslim (among others) insists that you and I possess the ability within ourselves to live by the Truth and merit ultimate 'salvation', and then a Christian insists that these things can only be gifts of God's grace, it raises a problem you could respond to in one of two ways. On the one hand, you could explore the grounds for these respective claims, and assess whether you personally have the capacity spoken of by Buddhism and Islam. Much easier than all this, however, is the 'economy of effort' approach: decide that both are true in some mysterious way.

To offer a more pointed example: when a Christian affirms that Jesus died on a cross and rose to life, and a Muslim insists that Jesus did neither of these, it produces a dilemma that you can approach in one of two ways. On the one hand, you could look into it for yourself, assessing what historians think happened to Jesus. (There are more books on questions like this than you probably imagine.) Easier by far, however, would be to accept both claims as true in their own way. While this would require a degree of 'mental elasticity' on your part – since in reality Jesus either did or did not die and rise again – it is clearly the option requiring the least effort.

What I'm suggesting here – and hopefully not too impolitely – is that our society's keenness to affirm all religious viewpoints stems, in part, from an aversion to having to think too deeply about any one of them. Put another way, the 'all roads lead to Rome' view of spirituality can be simply a way of justifying our own unwillingness to look down any of the roads.

And the result of this 'economy of effort' is rather sad. Whether by an aversion to intolerance or a tendency to take the easy option, this vague affirmation of all beliefs has the potential to leave us without faith altogether. English critic and author G. K. Chesterton once wrote:

> *An open mind is like an open mouth: its purpose is to bite on something nourishing. Otherwise, it becomes like a sewer, accepting everything, rejecting nothing* (Collected Works vol.16, 212).

As I've said several times before, my purpose in writing this book has not been to shine the light on one religion over another but to present all five in the best light I can. I close the book by urging spectators to keep exploring the big ideas that have shaped the world's civilizations. The 'economy of effort' approach to religion is a little like Chesterton's all-accepting mouth. But we do not honour the religions by affirming their sameness. We honour them by understanding their distinctive flavours and scrutinizing their central claims. It is in doing this that we may actually find ourselves able to 'bite on something nourishing'.

Glossary

Agni – Hindu god of fire

Amidah – Jewish *eighteen prayers*

Apostle – *one who is sent out* – Jesus chose twelve apostles who were given the special function to act in his name

Arhat – Buddhist – worthy one who has achieved a state of *karma-less* perfection

Ascetic – one who denies earthly comforts in an effort to strive for mystic consciousness

Atheist – one who believes that God does not exist

Atman – the Hindu soul

Atonement – Jewish concept of God's judgment falling on a sacrificed animal instead of on the person who has disobeyed God

Avatars – incarnations of various Hindu gods

Baptism – Christian cleansing ritual / spiritual bath symbolizing the removal of guilt from the believer and providing admission into the Christian church

Bar/bat Mitzvah – Jewish ceremony to mark the transition of a teenager into adulthood

Bhagavad-gita – *the Song of the Lord* – treasured Hindu text from *the Great epic of the Bharata Dynasty*

Bhakti yoga – Hindu path of devotion

Bodhi tree – *tree of wisdom* where Buddha discovered enlightenment

Bodhisattva – a Buddha-to-be, or one who delays attainment of *Nirvana* in order to assist others

Brahman – Hindu concept – the ultimate and only reality of the universe. All things originate from Brahman

Caliph – Islamic term given to the leader, or deputy, following the death of the prophet Muhammad

Devas – powerful unpredictable beings of the Hindu Vedas

Dharma – Hindu duty

Dvija – Hindu *twice-born* ceremony

Essenes – ultra-devout Jews around the first century who saw themselves as the true people of God. They lived in the desert and diligently followed the Scriptures and kept to the Jewish Law.

Eucharist – *Communion or Lord's Supper* – re-enacted meal of Jesus' 'Last Supper' with his disciples. The bread and the wine serve as a reminder of Jesus' death and resurrection

Gentiles – non Jews

Gospel – *grand news* – the New Testament first-century accounts of the life of Jesus

Grace – Christian emphasis on the unmerited gift of God's pardon

Hadiths – collection of the words and deeds of Muhammad

Hajj – Muslim pilgrimage to Mecca

Hanukkah – Jewish festival to mark rededication of the temple by Judas Maccabeus in 164 BC after successful Jewish revolt against Hellenistic rule

Hasmonean dynasty – century-long dynasty of Jewish priest-kings ruling Jerusalem as a free and autonomous state

Hellenistic empire – Greek empire under Alexander the Great and his successors

Imam – Sh'ite Muslim term for a leader thought to be able to intercede with Allah on behalf of a believer

Indra – Hindu warrior god

Islam – submission – surrendering your life to Allah

Jihad – Muslim concept of striving for Allah

Jnana yoga – Hindu path of knowledge

Karma (Buddhist) – wilful action growing out of desire

Karma (Hindu) – actions that determine future existence

Karma yoga – Hindu path of duties

Koran – (Quran) – holy book of Islam

Krishna – incarnation of Hindu god Vishnu

Mahabharata – epic Hindu poem of Bharata Dynasty

Mahayana Buddhism – *Great Vehicle* – dominant in Tibet, China, Japan and Korea

Majjhima Patipada – middle path of the Buddha

Manu (*Laws of*) – text outlining details of duties of various castes of Hindu society

Margas – paths to escape birth and rebirth

Messiah – 'anointed one' – Jewish belief in the future ultimate and eternal king by whose reign Israel would achieve its purpose

Midrash – Jewish written works devoted to interpreting sections of the Tanak – recasting old texts to have contemporary significance

Mishnah – recorded sayings and legal opinions of first- and second-century rabbis regarded as preserving the spoken instructions to Moses

Moksha – Hindu escape into ultimate reality

Monotheism – belief in *one* God

Muslim – one who submits to Allah

Nirvana – Buddhist notion of extinguishing of all desire – *blowing out* or *extinction*

Palestine – Roman name for land of Israel

Pantheism – everything is god

Pharisees – reform movement in Judaism around first century stressing commitment to preserving and obeying the Law

Pluralism – belief that spiritual truth is *plural* in form not singular

Polytheism – belief in a great number of gods

Protestantism – Christian churches derived from the sixteenth-century protest movement against the Roman Catholic Church's perceived abuses.

Ramayana – *Romance of Rama* – epic poem of Hindu Smriti writings

Sadducees – faction of conservative Jews under Roman rule – rejected innovation of faith and sought to maintain role of priest and temple. Religious aristocracy in Jerusalem

Saivism – devotion to Hindu god Siva

Samsara – Hindu notion of entrapment in birth, death and rebirth

Sanatana dharma – *Hinduism* or eternal law/religion

Sangha – the Buddhist community

Scruti – 'heard' writings of Hinduism

Sharia – Muslim concept of God's law

Shema – Jewish three-line statement of belief

Siddhartha Gautama – founder of Buddhism

Sira – first biography of Muhammad's life

Smriti – 'remembered' writings of Hinduism

Soma – Hindu god associated with key Vedic ritual

Sunna – the *example* of the prophet Muhammad

Talmud – Jewish set of books interpreting the Mishnah

Theravada Buddhism – *School of the Elders* – 'classical' Buddhism, found mainly in Sri Lanka, Laos, Cambodia, Thailand and Myanmar (Burma)

Torah – Sacred writing of Judaism – God's instruction to the Israelites on legal, environmental, religious and social matters. Came to refer specifically to first five books of the Jewish Bible

Transubstantiation – Roman Catholic belief that in the ritual of *the Lord's Supper* the bread and wine change substance and actually become the body and blood of Jesus

Trinity – Christian doctrine of one God in three persons – the Father, Son and Holy Spirit

Upanishads – sacred writings of Hinduism composed between 1000 and 300 BC

Vaishnavism – Hindu devotion to Vishnu

Varnas – Hindu castes

Vedas – earliest writings of Hinduism

Vedism – Aryan religion originally from Persia

Yom Kippur (Day of Atonement) – Jewish festival celebrating the mercy of God toward Israel

Zealots – Jewish faction violently opposed to Roman rule in the holy land

Zen Buddhism – extension of meditative dimension of Buddhism

Zionism – movement within Judaism for a Jewish state in the 'holy land'

Index

L
Lord's Supper 155–156
Love ethic 153–155

M
Maccabeus, Judas 105
Mahabharata 40
Mahayana (Great Vehicle) Buddhism 80–84
    Scriptures 80
    Lotus Sutra 81
    and Theravada Buddhism 80–82
    Nirvana 82
    Boddhisattva-path 82–83
    and Christianity 212
Mecca 173–174, 176–177, 178–179, 199–202
Medina 177–178
Meditation 75–77
Messiah 98–100, 151, 213
Modern Judaisms 92, 120–125
    Reform 121
    Orthodox 122
    Conservative 122–123
    Zionism 123–125
Midrash 112–113
Mishnah 111–112, 126
    in Modern Judaism 121–123
Moses 95–96
Muhammad
    life of 172–182
    sources about 172–173

N
New Testament 132–133, 147–148, 149
Nirvana 58
    and Third Noble Truth 68–70
    and Fourth Noble Truth 71
    and meditation 76
    in Theravada Buddhism 79

O
Orthodox Church 161–163

P
Passover (Pessah) 95–96
    and Exodus 95–96
    in Interim Judaism 104, 108
    in Classical Judaism 114
    death of Jesus 141–142
Path
    Middle – Majjhima Patipada 58
    of duties (karma-yoga) 44–45
    of knowledge (jnana-yoga) 45–46
    of devotion (bhakti-yoga) 46–47